AF882567

Open House West:
Museum Architecture and Changing Civic Identity

For their unwaivering committment to inspiring and mentoring the museum professional of the future, the Museum Studies class of 2000 wishes to dedicate this catalogue to Dr. Selma Holo and Jennifer Jaskowiak.

Fisher Gallery, University of Southern California
March 10 - April 24, 1999

Open House West:
Museum Architecture and Changing Civic Identity

Curatorial Advisor
Selma Holo

Curators
Katrina Ampil Bagaybagayan
Susana Bautista
Susan M. Kahn
Karen Lansky
Claudia A. Leos
Ariadni Ariane Liokatis
Susan Camille Passow
Karen Weldon Roswell

Technical Editor
Max F. Schulz

Exhibition Coordinator
Jennifer Jaskowiak

A collaboration with
USC School of Architecture

© 1999 Fisher Gallery, University of Southern California
University Park, Los Angeles, CA 90089-0292
ISBN: 0-945192-22-3
Library of Congress Catalog Card Number: 98-89618

All rights reserved. No part of this catalog may be reproduced in any form by electronic means, including information storage and retrieval systems, without permission in writing from the Fisher Gallery except by a reviewer who may quote brief passages in review.

Design and Production
Sibylle Hagmann, *Graphic Designer, USC School of Architecture*
Karen Weldon Roswell, *USC Museum Studies Program*

Copy Editor
Susan M. Kahn, *USC Museum Studies Program*

Printer
Typecraft, Inc., Pasadena

Fisher Gallery Staff
Selma Holo, *Director*
Kay Allen, *Associate Director*
Max F. Schulz, *Curator*
Jennifer Jaskowiak, *Curator/Exhibitions Coordinator*
Jeanette LaVere, *Education Coordinator*
William Vaughan, *Preparator*
Gymeka Williams, *Administrative and Public Relations Assistant*

USC Architectural Guild Press
This catalog is partially funded by a grant from the Edna Blurock Publication Fund of the University of Southern California School of Architecture.

Table of Contents

Acknowledgements

The Museum Studies class of 2000 would like to take the opportunity to acknowledge the individuals and institutions that made possible the conception and completion of this exhibition.

To Dr. Selma Holo, Director of the Museum Studies Program and the Fisher Gallery, we owe our deepest thanks for her insight and wisdom. Without the perseverance and patience of Jennifer Jaskowiak, Curator and Exhibitions Coordinator, we could never have seen our vision come to completion. Only through the guidance of Kay Allen, Associate Director, were we able to find the resources necessary to make this exhibition a reality. Jeanette LaVere, Educator, has shown us how to make the exhibition meaningful to our visitors, an increasingly important pursuit in museum work. We are also grateful to Gymeka Williams, Administrative Assistant, for her organizational skills, which proved to be vital to the coordination of a project of this scale. For his unique talent for producing tangible realities from our ideas, we owe many thanks to Preparator, William Vaughan.

We wish to extend our gratitude to James M. Steele, Associate Professor of Architecture, whose imparted knowledge and expertise gave us the confidence to write the catalogue essays. The enthusiastic support of Robert H. Timme, Della and Harry Mac Donald Dean, School of Architecture, has guided our planning of this exhibition from the earliest stages. Deepest thanks must be given to Dr. Max Schulz, Distinguished Emeritus Professor of English, whose tireless efforts and careful editing have guided so many students over the years. The artistic vision and energy of Sibylle Hagmann created a lasting document of our labors. Thanks, also, to the experts who graciously contributed essays: Wim de Wit, The Getty Center, R. Doss Mabe, Zimmer, Gunsul, Frasca; and Charles A. Lagreco, USC School of Architecture.

We are especially thankful to those institutions that provided the basis for our exhibition and the staff members who facilitated its organization: the Phoenix Art Museum, James Ballinger, Director; the Museum of Contemporary Art, Richard Koshalek, Director; The Centro Cultural de Tijuana, Mexico, Mrs. Irma de la Cruz de Larroque, Director of Public Relations; the Seattle Art Museum, Gail E. Joice, Senior Deputy Director; the Museum of Contemporary Art, San Diego, Hugh Davies, Director; the San Francisco Museum of Modern Art, David Ross, Director; the Skirball Cultural Center, Dr. Uri Herscher, President and CEO; the California Science Center, Jeffrey Rudolph, Executive Director; and the Getty Center, Barry Munitz, CEO.

Special thanks are due to the architects and firms who so generously shared models, plans, drawings, and photographs, and contributed in countless other ways. We would like to acknowledge: Tod Williams, Billie Tsien and Associates; Mr. Manuel Rosen Morrison, FAIA; Venturi, Scott Brown and Associates; Olson & Sundberg Architects, Inc.; the Architectural Offices of Mario Botta; Bechtel Civil Engineering; Moshe Safdie and Associates; David R. Singer, Architect; Peretti and Park; Richard Meier & Partners; and the Zimmer, Gunsul, Frasca Partnership.

The following individuals made generous contributions to the development of the project: Margaret McLaughlin, Professor at USC's Annenberg School of Communication and Interactive Art Museum Investigator; Mark Bielak, Director of USC's Multimedia University Academy; John Meunier, Dean of the School of Architecture, Arizona State University; David Fuggins; Elba Bautista-Smith; Kathleen M. Weldon; Patrick T. Wynne; Gia Bagaybagayan; Mia Bagaybagayan; Rick Meade.

The continued support of Dr. Morton O. Schapiro, Dean of the College of Letters, Arts, and Sciences, has helped produce a thriving Museum Studies Program at USC. Finally, we owe a sincere appreciation to the faculty of the Department of Art History in the College of Letters, Arts and Sciences, and the chair, Dr. Gordon Berger. Their focus on scholarship has immersed us in the complexitites of art historical research and provided us with the knowledge so vital to the museum professionals of the future.

Preface

Open House West: Museum Architecture and Changing Civic Identity is a multi-faceted celebration. First and foremost, it is an exhibition that celebrates the University of Southern California's Museum Studies Program students. As Art History M.A. candidates who are receiving advanced training for the museum profession, these students typically spend three semesters developing and producing an exhibition for USC's Fisher Gallery. *Open House West* is the culmination of that curatorial research and catalogue preparation, but it is also a demonstration of their newly acquired skills in the other significant duties of a museum professional today, including educational programming, fundraising, and installation. As their curatorial advisor, I can attest to their having acquired the expertise that will allow them to take on similar responsibilities as they move from graduate school to internships at museums throughout the nation, and ultimately to responsible and influential positions as museum curators, educators, and administrators.

Open House West is also a celebration of the Museum Studies Program's special relationship with the USC School of Architecture. Dean Robert Timme and I have worked together now for two years, encouraging our students of museology to consider the world of museums in the context of architecture and its impact. Art historians all, they emerge from these experiences with perspectives broadened and assumptions challenged. While our exhibition last year examined architecture as artistic subject, this year it investigates architecture as principal vehicle for the redefinition of a meaningful civic context. Our collaborations with the School of Architecture have resulted in exciting and stimulating intellectual events, not only at the academic level, but also for our many visitors who come to USC Fisher Gallery with their wide ranging interests. I am extremely grateful to Dean Timme, his faculty and staff, as they have contributed immeasurably to this exhibitions success.

That USC's support of our interdisciplinary efforts has been broad based and unstinting is evidenced in the College of Letters, Arts and Sciences, which has contributed fund for the realization of *Open House West.* In Art History itself I remember warmly a conversation with the Chair, Nancy Troy, in which she suggested that museums and their buildings might be a topic for a museum studies exhibition. I later developed that idea with James Steele, professor in the School of Architecture. The work of our students was then supplemented by scholars and architects outside of the immediate USC community. I am grateful that Wim de Wit at the Getty Center and R. Doss Mabe at Zimmer Gunsul Frasca have seen fit to write for our project and to help us take a more expansive view of the museological phenomenon. They, along with Victoria Newhouse and Michael Palladino, who participated in the KCRW interview with me, have added new dimensions to our thinking.

Of course, what we are all celebrating, as well, is an exciting moment for museums up and down the west coast. From Tijuana to Seattle, new and remodeled structures have sprung up in the last few years. Without pretending to have included even a majority of those buildings in our exhibition, the Museum Studies class has chosen a representative few to indicate the energy and variety behind that surge. The students have constructed a frame in which the civic context of each museum building, previously only analyzed individually, can be set. They have pointed to a regional phenomenon. Then, the context having been established, they have tried to ask the hard questions about whether the architecture has enabled or hindered each museum's guiding mission. Every contributor to the catalogue, whether student or practicing professional, has tried to go beyond a mere discussion of bricks and mortar to locate the identity and urban issues that drove the creation of their museums.

Finally, we are celebrating the directors and curators; and of course, the architects of all of the museums included in this exhibition. They, in the true spirit of inquiry and collegiality, allowed us to borrow models, to reproduce photographs, and to interview them endlessly. *Open House West* would never have been possible without their cooperation.

Selma Holo
Director
Museum Studies Program and
USC Fisher Gallery

Preface

The School of Architecture at the University of Southern California is proud to be associated with the Fisher Gallery and the Museum Studies Program on this very significant project, *Open House West: Museum Architecture and Changing Civic Identity*. The show is a clear illustration of the new responsibilities that museums are assuming in our society. Not since the late nineteenth century, when the British developed a series of museums and galleries to present artistic, scientific, and cultural artifacts to an emerging middle-class population has such a redefinition occurred in the role of the museum. What is also comparable between today's museums and the museums of the 1800s is the quality of architecture that emerged in order to facilitate this significant urban building type. Alfred Waterhouse designed the colorful, terra-cotta, Romanesque Natural History Museum in London, Sir John Soane developed the magnificent light-filled rooms of the Dulwich Picture Gallery, and Robert Smirke created the culturally defining, neo-classical British Museum. The projects presented in *Open House West* are of equivalent seminal importance to the late twentieth century as were those antecedents to the nineteenth. The difference is, however, in the activities of the museums. Today's new museums have become places of entertainment, education, socialization, and cultural identification. They foster a sense of pride for their communities, create identity for their cities, and generate economic benefits through jobs and cultural tourism. This distinction, while of some interest to the viewer, is of paramount importance to the Museum Studies Program students whose training is preparing them for professions in such facilities.

Open House West has been made rich by the range of participants who lent their expertise to the work. Architects, curators, museum directors, faculty, and students have spent the past year discussing and writing about the issues that informed the design directions of these important institutions. The spirit of exploration and discovery that brought all of these individuals together is evident in this catalog, presenting student articles alongside the writings of faculty, curators, and architects. Although a student show, the museum study students have achieved in *Open House West* a level of quality that is clearly professional. It is particularly of interest that this collection of emerging new museums as selected by the students and presented in the show provides an indication of the diverse careers that are possible for these student curators upon graduation—what an exciting prospect for the future.

This show is the second collaboration between the Fisher Gallery and the School of Architecture. It is an example of the level of success that can be achieved when different units work together on interdisciplinary explorations. It is noteworthy that neither of these entities could have achieved such a sterling exhibition on its own. *Open House West* is also a part of 1999 USC Festival of the Arts entitled, *Arts and the Thematic Experience*. The Festival is a joint series of projects of the schools of Architecture, Fine Arts, Music, and Theater as well as the Fisher Gallery. The collaborative effort is a result of the University of Southern California's recently announced "Arts Initiative," an integral component of the University's strategic plan developed by President Steven B. Sample and Senior Vice President and Provost Lloyd Armstrong, Jr.

Fisher Gallery and its Director Selma Holo and the student curators of *Open House West: Museum Architecture and Changing Civic Identity* are to be applauded for selecting this timely topic, and for achieving such a successful exhibition. The show leaves little doubt that the new museums of the west coast are emerging as significant elements of the urban fabric, important components in the future of our cities and in the changing concept of civic identity.

Robert H. Timme, FAIA
Della and Harry McDonald Dean
School of Architecture

What Museums Have Been, What They Are Becoming

Wim de Wit

When The Museums Were White: A Study of the Museum as Building Type

In the early 1980s, a group of Los Angeles collectors interested in contemporary art took the initiative to establish a museum dedicated exclusively to the collection and display of contemporary art. They raised $23 million, found a downtown site on Bunker Hill in a new development of offices, stores, apartment buildings, and hotels, and hired the eminent Japanese architect Arata Isozaki to design the new museum. Ground was broken in late 1983 and construction was expected to take about three years. However, the museum staff, led first by Pontus Hulten (of Centre Pompidou fame) and very soon thereafter by the current director, Richard Koshalek, did not want to wait three years to organize their first exhibition. Instead, in a conscious attempt to sustain the excitement and momentum created during the initial fund drive, they decided to open a temporary museum as soon as possible in two old, industrial buildings in an area called Little Tokyo, just east of downtown Los Angeles. Renovated by well-known architect Frank Gehry, the Temporary Contemporary as it was then called (now the Geffen Contemporary) was an instant success. Audiences liked its informality and unpretentiousness: people felt, and still feel, at home in the wide open spaces that seem to have no design to them; they feel comfortable with the open trusses under the roof that are not hidden behind a dropped ceiling; and, they admire Gehry's trademark steel and chain-link canopy, which marks the entrance. In short, it is the seeming absence of design that made the building so popular (fig. 1).

Fig. 1 The Geffen Contemporary, Los Angeles; interior.

Isozaki's Museum of Contemporary Art (MOCA, fig. 2) building did not elicit such a positive reception when it opened in late 1986. A review of the literature suggests that while the museum trustees wanted a famous architect to design their building, they may also have been somewhat uncomfortable with the end product that would result. They wanted a building that, at least inside, would be totally neutral: clean, white rooms that would respect the art to be displayed there. Critics, however, have stated that the galleries, while graced by pleasing proportions and excellent light, are somewhat boring in their lack of articulation and ornamentation.

These responses to two related buildings testify to the complexity of a problem that every architect and museum director face and that is referred to by almost every critic reviewing a new museum building, namely, what role architectural design can or should play in the production of an art museum space. The question can also be worded in another way: is the architect, who is as much an artist as any sculptor or painter, to be permitted to create a building that not only works well functionally, but also incorporates his or her ideas of what architecture can and should be; alternatively, is the architect, having been commissioned to design an art museum or gallery, compelled to relinquish any personal vision, and restrict her/himself to building little more than a box in which art can be displayed to best advantage? What this question ultimately comes down to is this: does architectural expression tend to overwhelm art, or can architecture and art co-exist and complement each other? This question has been asked repeatedly in the last twenty-five years in relation to Renzo Piano and Richard Rogers's Centre Pompidou in Paris (1971-1977), Gae Aulenti's Musée d'Orsay, also in Paris (1980-1986), I. M. Pei's East Building of the National Gallery of Art in Washington, D.C. (1978), James Stirling and Michael Wilford's Neue Staatsgalerie in Stuttgart (1977-1984), and most pointedly with regard to the Groninger Museum in Groningen, the Netherlands, designed by Italian architect, Alessandro Mendini, in collaboration with Philippe Starck, Michele de Lucchi, and Coop Himmelb(l)au (1988-1992), to name just a few recently completed museum buildings.

To those with passing interest in the relationship between architectural criticism and museum architecture, it may seem that this conundrum has been around as long as museums have been in existence. That is, however, a misconception. In fact, the issue has a shorter pedigree, having been raised to prominence only in the years since Modernism was introduced in museum architecture. Modernist structures of steel, glass, and white-washed concrete were considered to be sufficiently neutral to allow for the showing of any kind of art. The impact of the Modernist movement and of the formal vocabulary typical of it was so strong that for a time no other kind of museum environment could be imagined. Changes in the physical characteristics of art works and in the means of their production also contributed greatly to the development of a new attitude with regard to museum architecture. In order to appreciate the reasons for this change, it is helpful to examine the history of the museum as building type.

As many recent studies of the history of collecting and display have shown, museums in the early modern period evolved from collections of art objects or collections of curiosa (also called *Wunderkammer*) that had originally been housed in private settings and were subsequently made accessible to a larger public. This transition took place in the second half of the eighteenth century when noble or royal families, influenced by enlightened thinking of the time, concentrated their sometimes vast collections in a refurbished palace or villa and opened them to the public. In this way, a public- spirited nobleman or king could display generosity, share his wealth with "the people," and give expression to the idea of *egalité*—without actually relinquishing any personal property. Architecturally, these early museums retained their original residential character. Floor plans were scarcely changed, if at all, to deal with the fact that groups of visitors were expected. In general, the only adjustment made was a lavish redecoration of the rooms to create what were then considered to be appropriate decorative settings for the art and to give expression to the importance of the family that owned this art.

Diverse collections of works of art were opened up everywhere, the most famous of which was probably the Louvre in Paris. However, amongst princely palaces and their collections, the Villa Borghese in Rome is perhaps more revealing of how architectural solutions were achieved and what role the architect played in that process. The paintings and sculpture in the Villa Borghese were originally assembled in the early seventeenth century as a semipublic collection by Cardinal Scipione Borghese, the nephew of Pope Paul V. The collection was converted into a public museum in the 1780s and 1790s by Prince Marcantonio Borghese, who hired Antonio Asprucci and his son, Mario Asprucci, among others, as the architects to transform the Villa's rooms into galleries. Each hall was decorated in a style understood as supportive of the art objects to be shown in it. Ceilings were decorated with large paintings, doors were surrounded by heavy frames, and the wall surfaces were subdivided into smaller framed panels containing mural paintings or sculptural reliefs. Some of these designs by the Aspruccis and their colleagues were quite elaborate and, according to what can be gleaned from the drawings, not all of them were executed. Several of the decorations for the so-called Egyptian Room, for example, were replaced by more modest designs (fig. 3). Prohibitively high costs were probably the main reason for modifying this part of the elaborate redecoration. Fear that the art on display would be overwhelmed by the art on the walls did not appear to have been a major concern in the eighteenth century.

Over the course of the next century and a half, as collections created by the nobility were transformed into the first public museums, the palatial buildings housing them

Fig. 2 The Museum of Contemporary Art, Los Angeles; entrance court and library wing.

Fig. 3 Tomaso Conca, unexecuted design for the descoration of a wall in the Egyptian Room in the Villa Borghese, ca. 1778-1779; watercolor over graphite.

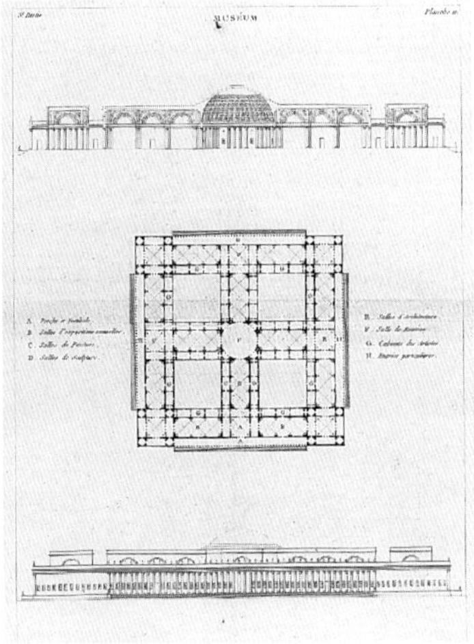

Fig. 4 J. N. L. Durand, "Muséum," engraving by C. Normand in J. N. L. Durand Précis des Leçons d'Architecture donnés à l'Ecole Royale Polytechnique, *vol. 3, plate 11.*

became extremely influential in the development of the museum building as a type. Its long corridors with adjacent spacious rooms were very appropriate for the display of paintings and sculpture in chronological order and organized by school; each group of artists could be shown in its own room. The Louvre was one of the earliest museums in which art was organized in this didactic way and in which the building's spatial layout lent itself to such a display. As Carol Duncan noted in her book *Civilizing Rituals: Inside Public Art Museums*:

> *In a relatively short time, the Louvre's directors (drawing partly on German and Italian precedents) worked out a whole set of practices that came to characterize art museums everywhere. In short, the museum organized its collections into art-historical schools and installed them so as to make visible the development and achievement of each school.*[1]

The Louvre was also influential with regard to another important feature of museum design: the lighting of the galleries. It was in this building that architects and those responsible for the installation of the art first experimented with light entering the rooms from above, through skylights. Lighting in a museum building, like acoustics in a concert hall, is one of the determining factors for the functional success of the space and for that reason the issue of illumination of galleries remains almost as controversial as the role of architectural expression in a space devoted to the exhibition of works of art.

Museum architecture exemplified by the Louvre became a general prototype through the agency of J. N. L. Durand, architectural theoretician and professor at the École Polytechnique in Paris. In his book *Précis des Leçons d'Architecture* (1802-1805), Durand illustrated and described what he recommended to his students as the ideal floor plan for a museum building (fig. 4). While on the one hand harking back to similar designs by contemporaries of Durand's master Etienne-Louis Boullée,[2] in plan Durand's building showed many similarities to the Louvre. Durand's museum was a huge square block with long corridors running along the perimeter and giving access to relatively small rooms. Inside this square was a Greek cross built up similarly out of corridors and small galleries. At the center of the cross and thus the center of the entire museum was a circular space covered by a dome. The four courtyards created by the cross inside the square were kept uncovered. This plan had enormous appeal for the architectural world because of its symmetry—an organizing feature typical of most Beaux-Arts designs of the nineteenth and early twentieth centuries—and because of specific advantages resulting from the modularity of the design, which meant that the large square block could easily be divided into half blocks or quarter blocks according to the funds available, while keeping the option open for additional parts to be built later. It appealed no less to the museum world, as the long corridors of this plan made it possible to present the works of art in an educationally driven way, one that followed a chronological order rather than, for example, an iconographical method. The flexibility of this plan is further suggested by the fact that Durand did not indicate what the interiors of the corridors and galleries in his museum building should look like. As for illumination, that was supposed to come into the galleries through semicircular clerestory windows placed directly below the vaulted roofs.

Examples of Durand's museum type can be found everywhere. The best known of the early nineteenthth century is probably the Altes Museum in Berlin, designed by Karl F. Schinkel (1823-1828). Its floor plan is half a "Durand plan": a rectangle consisting of galleries placed around the perimeter with a huge domed atrium space connecting the two long sides of the rectangle and creating two courts inside the rectangle. The central atrium space is the most elaborately decorated of all the rooms: its coffered Pantheon-like dome is lit by a skylight and its columns support a second floor walkway around the atrium's perimeter. The galleries were relatively simple in design and were originally organized according to a strictly historical progression. As Nikolaus Pevsner noted in his book *A History of Building Types*, the desire for a complete historical overview was so strong that Karl Wilhelm von Humboldt, the philologist and statesman who chaired the commission responsible for determining the display in the museum galleries, proposed that gaps in the collection would be filled by copies—something quite acceptable for sculpture collections (where plaster casts of famous pieces of sculpture were often highly valued) but rather radical when it came to collections of paintings.[3] Certainly from a late twentieth-century perspective it is not surprising that the commission's proposal on this point was not accepted.

Humboldt was not alone, however, in advocating the need to provide a survey of art history through a linear, historical arrangement of the collections. The great majority of museums built in the nineteenth and first half of the twentieth centuries followed this principle, which was first articulated by Durand and then ingeniously materialized by Schinkel. The list of museums laid out according to this plan is endless. Indeed, every museum designed by an architect with Beaux-Arts training is rectangular in shape with the entrance in the middle of the long side of the rectangle. Once inside, the visitor can choose to go left or right and proceed in either case into an enfilade of galleries that will lead him or her through the entire museum. The link connecting the two long sides is made in some cases by a gallery showing highlights from the collection, in other instances by a gallery for changing exhibitions, and on yet other occasions by a formal stair to the second floor. While this museum type can be found all over the world, it became especially popular in the United States, where Beaux-Arts trained architects designed most of the museums in the late nineteenth and early twentieth centuries. Examples range from the Museum of Fine Arts in Boston (1906-1931), to the Cleveland Museum of Art (1916), and to the National Gallery of Art in Washington, D.C. (1941). Even such a museum as the Corcoran in Washington, D.C. (Ernest Flagg, 1893-1895), despite its regular site plan, is laid out according to this principle. One of the last museums in this series is the Solomon R. Guggenheim Museum in New York (1943-1959) in which Frank Lloyd Wright, as indicated by Helen Searing in her book *New American Art Museums*,[4] took the Beaux-Arts circular atrium space as the essence of the museum building and constructed the surrounding processional display spaces as a single spiraling ramp rising above the central void. By placing the gallery spaces on the ramp along the perimeter of the atrium space, Wright made the visitor's progress through his museum even more linear than any of the Beaux-Arts museum buildings ever could have done.

Classical as far as the sources of their designs are concerned, all of these museums were rather moderately decorated inside. There might be a frieze along the upper part of a wall or a molding around a wall surface in order to frame the pieces to be hung on that wall; otherwise, the decoration of the interiors is generally quite restrained. This is not the case with many nineteenth-century museum buildings that were Neo-Gothic in style. Those buildings possessed a profusion of ornamentation that is now almost impossible to imagine for exhibition spaces. One of the most beautiful examples is the University Museum at Oxford University designed by Thomas Deane and Benjamin Woodward in 1855-1860. Conceived on a square plan, the museum consists basically of one huge hall surrounded by auditorium, class room, and office spaces. The exhibition hall is extremely impressive. Designed with a great deal of input by John Ruskin, the art and architecture critic and social reformer,[5] the hall features a huge glass roof supported by slender columns and iron arches. The decoration of the capitals and arches with reference to plant life in England is particularly stunning. While we are dealing here with a museum of natural history rather than an art museum, it is nonetheless interesting that nobody at the time the museum was built deemed its extensive decoration to be inappropriate for a museum. Critical reviews of the building, especially by Ruskin himself, were not entirely favorable on architectural grounds; however, the suitability of this space as an exhibition gallery was never questioned.

Another potent example of a museum with many Neo-Gothic references in its decoration is the Rijksmuseum in Amsterdam, the Netherlands, designed by architect Petrus J. H. Cuypers between 1876 and 1885. Like many of the museums mentioned above, the Rijksmuseum was established to house the Dutch national and royal collections and its floor plan closely follows the Beaux-Arts model. Rectangular in plan, the Rijksmuseum has two courtyards separated by a gallery for old masters. The rest of the galleries are laid out along the perimeter of the rectangular block and are purposely arranged in such manner that a visitor can experience the works of art as a progressive historical lesson about the greatness of Holland's past.[6] In spite of this classical, conceptual armature, Cuypers's decoration of the interiors of stair halls, galleries, and corridors was far from Beaux-Arts in style. These rooms had polychrome decoration achieved through the use of colored bricks and mural paintings that supported the museum's programmatic display showing Holland's greatness. This decoration thus had an educational purpose and initially it was greatly appreciated. By the 1920s and 1930s when concepts of exhibiting art changed radically, the decorations were perceived as too overbearing, with a negative impact on the art, and were therefore completely removed soon after the Second World War.

When the Rijksmuseum's interiors lost their colorful ornamentation, the museum joined many others that experienced a similar architectural transformation. Indeed, museums all over Europe and the United States were whitewashed in the 1940s and 1950s as the culmination of a trend that had started in the 1910s to modernize both museum practice and the display environment. The museum's original function of storeroom-cum-gallery-of-art where amateur and specialist alike could study the history of art by viewing paintings and sculpture in a strictly historical arrangement was under increasing pressure as the museum gradually developed into a place where curators were no longer caretakers but scholars in a specific period or aspect of the history of art. For a variety of reasons, scholar-curators saw their task as the education of the public through temporary exhibitions focused on specialized topics with carefully chosen objects. Exhibition galleries were therefore no longer static spaces in which the same works of art were shown year after year. Museums required flexible spaces without ornamentation that might be appropriate to one exhibition but clash with the next. The generally accepted classical layout of the art museum plan needed to be rethought and revised.

After the turn of the century, Alfred Lichtwark, the director of the Kunsthalle in Hamburg, was one of several theoreticians writing about the need to reconceptualize the museum building. Already in the early 1910s, Lichtwark had pointed out that not only a new architecture was being developed without the usual references to historic styles, but also the function of the museum was changing. He rejected as outdated the museum that resembled a palace with its impressive colonnaded façade, imposing staircase, and enfilade of rooms that could be enjoyed by only a relatively small group of connoisseurs.

> *[The museum] does not want to be just a storage facility* (Speicher) *any more; instead, it wants to make its possessions useful through tasteful exhibitions. It does not want to be just a promenade where one goes for a walk either, but wants to lure people to come and stay in a pleasant environment. It now tends to use reading rooms, study halls, and auditoriums, as well as many other additional spaces, which were unimaginable at the time that the first museum buildings of the twentieth century were built.*[7]

Clearly influenced by rationalist thinking about architecture, Lichtwark promoted a museum building that would be designed according to its function rather than according to a pre-existing building type, especially one that, in Lichtwark's opinion, was developed primarily as a place to show off the prosperity of a country or city, and was not attractive to anyone other than out-of-town visitors who had free time on their hands. Instead, Lichtwark's ideal museum consisted of long corridors that would function as thoroughfares and exhibition halls that could be entered from these corridors. Such an arrangement would separate the function of movement through a building from that of quietly viewing the works of art. For lighting of the galleries, Lichtwark preferred windows rather than skylights, but under no circumstance could the placement of the windows be determined by the composition of the façade. The façade should take shape as envelope around a functional arrangement of spaces and windows. The windows should be so placed as to achieve optimal results in the galleries, that is, they should leave ample space for the works of art on the walls and be placed sufficiently high in the gallery to illuminate the entire room.

Modernist architects of the early twentieth century must have felt comfortable with Lichtwark's proposals, which applied widely recognized Modernist principles to replace the traditional type of museum building. Dutch architect Hendrik P. Berlage demonstrated familiarity with Lichtwark's recommendations in his design for the Gemeentemuseum in The Hague (1919-1935).[8] Berlage's arrangement of the gallery spaces and corridors in this museum followed Lichtwark closely. At the same time, however, the spatial arrangement of a succession of small rectangular galleries was inflexible, and Berlage was not so devoted to Modernism that he would design a museum with completely white interiors. Indeed, the museum plan advocated by both Lichtwark and Berlage was, in fact, still closely related to the Beaux-Arts layout.

Ironically, when one compares the Gemeentemuseum's floor plan to that of Durand's ideal type, one notices few differences. The most significant change in museum design was catalyzed by developments in the sphere of commercial galleries and museums of modern art, which required spaces conducive to the display of ever larger paintings and pieces of sculpture. As the art market expanded and diversified, exhibition spaces had to become flexible to allow for a great variety of displays. The ideal solution was therefore the creation of large neutral spaces that could, when necessary, be subdivided according to the specific requirements of each exhibition. Consistent with the fundamental principles of Modernism, a minimally articulated architecture was seen as least obtrusive and therefore most desirable for showing art. Any ornamentation, such as moldings, paneling, or base boards, was out of the question for years, especially during the period in which pure and hardcore Modernism was sanctioned institutionally. In the 1980s, when its principles were opened to question, some of these decorative features were reintroduced, but usually in a subdued form. Clearly, the fear that architecture and its ornamental articulation might overwhelm art had not entirely disappeared.

The number of new art museums designed and built in the fifty years since the Second World War is as large as, or possibly even larger than, the number built in the preceding one hundred and fifty years. Every city that aspires to a place in the worlds of culture and mass tourism has built at least one museum in the last few decades. Very often the museum is designed by a well-known architect, who can give the city a "monument" that will attract not only the audiences for art, but also the ever growing audience for modern architecture. Many critics have pointed out that in the years since the Second World War the museum has taken over the position of the cathedral, or the opera house, or the philharmonic, as the locus in which a city's cultural ambitions are concentrated. A few examples will have to suffice to mark the parameters of this enormous force-field of change in which architectural types have proliferated. It is impossible to summarize all the characteristics that distinguish Louis Kahn's museum buildings, for example, from Philip Johnson's or Oscar Niemeyer's.

Perhaps the most important art museum of the mid-twentieth century was the Museum of Modern Art in New York, completed in 1939 according to the design of the architects Philip L. Goodwin and Edward Durrell Stone. A six-story highrise with a roofgarden on top, the MoMA building has since its inauguration[9] had large, open exhibition galleries that could be adjusted to specific curatorial needs. Both outside and inside, the architects of the MoMA building adhered strictly to the practices of Modernism as far as colors and materials were concerned: white walls, glass, and steel were abundantly present. MoMA became an example for many Modernist museum buildings of the 1940s and after.

The many museum renovations in Italy in the 1950s and 1960s present an interesting episode in the struggle to resolve the competing claims of museum architecture and the works of art exhibited in the galleries. Although clearly Modernist in their approach to temporary display and permanent exhibition space, these museums are housed in old palaces and monasteries, whose interiors had to be preserved rather than stripped of all their architectural details. The presence of obtrusive architectural elements that may clash with the art on the wall had to be accepted and, whenever possible, used to advantage. Such architects as Franco Albini and Carlo Scarpa came up with excellent solutions for the problem of how to show works of art in such a setting. In the Palazzo Abatellis in Palermo (1953), for example, Scarpa accepted the specific qualities of each room and showed as few objects as possible in beautiful spatial arrangements that not only draw the viewer's attention to the works, but also emphasize the architectural characteristics of the room. The room may not be as flexible as the modern taste of the era required, but the sparse arrangement of the objects on display nevertheless creates the same feeling.

Mies van der Rohe's Nationalgalerie in Berlin and Piano and Rogers's Centre Pompidou in Paris show two extreme solutions to the problem of design of an open, flexible gallery. The Nationalgalerie's design aims at achieving an elegant, temple-like building with two exhibition floors, one so open that its glass walls are transparent to onlookers, the other (located in the raised plinth of the building) invisible from the outside and surrounded by solid walls. Interrupted only by a few columns, the interior spaces are therefore flexible enough; but other considerations have arisen to impinge upon the success of the galleries. In the upper level, for example, the light levels near the windows are so high that one cannot show any art there; and whatever is exhibited near the perimeter needs to be turned away from the outside. On the other hand, the lower level gallery is experienced as a basement space and is therefore

Fig. 5 Groninger Museum, interior.

less desirable for exhibitions. Given the lack of flexibility that follows upon such problems as these, the Nationalgalerie's design has not found many followers.

The design of the Centre Pompidou aims at flexibility achieved by architecturally turning the building inside out. All structural, architectural, and utilitarian elements, such as stairs, columns, ducts, and pipes, have been removed from the interior and placed on the outside where they become the building's façade. The result on the interior is that the architects could create large floors with hardly any interruption of spatial flow. Yet, neither staff nor visitors feel very comfortable in the building's enormous exhibition spaces in which the noise levels are high and exposed structural elements and other industrial materials are often experienced as intrusive as well as hostile. Most visitors to the building do not actually visit the exhibitions, choosing instead only to ride the escalators that are a prominent feature of the museum's façade.

More recently, other museum buildings have questioned the Modernist idea of the white, flexible exhibition gallery in different ways. One example is the Groninger Museum in the Netherlands (1988-1992), the other is the Getty Museum in Los Angeles (completed in 1997).

When the city of Groningen and the director of the Groninger Museum, Frans Haks, decided to build a new museum, they went looking for an architect who through the design could give expression to the diverse character of the collection, which is composed of regional archaeological finds, Asian ceramics, pre-1950 art, and modern art. It was Haks's innovative idea to hire not one but a group of architects, who, under the direction of Milanese architect Alessandro Mendini, would each design a part of the museum. Architects Michele de Lucchi from Milan and Philippe Starck from Paris designed wings that stand out in the Dutch urban environment, but are not particularly innovative as far as the conceptualization of exhibition space is concerned. The Viennese firm, Coop Himmelb(l)au, however, designed a gallery for pre-1950 art that is completely new in its approach to the use of color and architectural detail inside the gallery. The gallery seems to be built of floating steel plates connected by glass windows. Inside is a bridge that spans the entire space enabling the visitor to gain an elevated perspective that is quite different from the straight-on view one has when walking in the gallery below (fig. 5). The colors of both the outside and the inside are also unheard of in the museum world. Bright reds and blues abound, and inside one can even see mottled surfaces. Coop Himmelb(l)au in this design no longer aims at creating a comfortable space for the display of many different kinds of art, but seeks to offer a new solution in which architecture and art are of equal value. In that sense, we have almost come full circle, back to the ideas embodied in the Villa Borghese.

The solution of the Getty Museum is very different. After the Trustees of the J. Paul Getty Trust had commissioned the architect Richard Meier to design six interconnected buildings, which were to include a museum, on top of a hill in West Los Angeles, the staff of the museum decided that Meier's Modernist approach would not be appropriate for the design of the museum's gallery spaces. Apparently, they feared that Meier's white, elegantly proportioned interiors would look too sterile for their collection of pre-1900 paintings and sculpture, illuminated manuscripts, drawings, and ornate decorative arts. Instead, they brought in an interior decorator based in New York, Thierry Despont, who designed distinctly Post-Modern, very colorful, and sometimes sensuously opulent interiors for the galleries. Many reviewers have noted that at the Getty Museum there is a very abrupt separation between exterior and interior sensibilities, but because the work of one designer does not spill over in that of the other, the two do not clash.

Not surprisingly, neither of these two museums is totally successful. In the six years since the opening of the Groninger Museum, the curators have not been able to satisfactorily install art in the Coop Himmelb(l)au gallery. And critics have said that in the Getty Museum there are certain galleries where the colorful textiles on the wall make the (less) colorful decorative art objects look faded and out of place. Both museums, however, exemplify a new trend away from the monumentality of the big white space in which each work of art is seen as a self-sufficient object demanding the viewer's full attention. The Groninger Museum and the Getty Museum (and Frank Gehry's critically acclaimed Guggenheim Museum in Bilbao, Spain, for that matter) seem to suggest that some curators and architects want to devise a gallery space in which the art together with the architecture create a total environment, conducive to contemplation of the ideas behind an assemblage of art objects. It is still too early to determine if this trend will take root.

I wish to thank Cara Mullio, Sandy Nairne, and Wolf Prix for their advice and suggestions. As always, I am extremely grateful to my wife, Nancy Troy, for her critical support.

1 Carol Duncan, *Civilizing Rituals: Inside Public Art Museums* (London, New York: Routledge, 1995), 24.

2 See Nikolaus Pevsner, *A History of Building Types* (London: Thames and Hudson, 1976), 118 and 122.

3 *Ibid.*, 126-128. The author gives a very informative overview of the design and installation histories of this museum.

4 Helen Searing, *New American Art Museums* (New York: Whitney Museum of Art in association with University of California Press, 1982), 53-56. See also "The Development of a Museum Typology," in *Museum News*, 65, no 4 (1987): 20-31, by the same author.

5 Eve Blau, *Ruskinian Gothic: The Architecture of Deane and Woodward, 1845-1861* (Princeton: Princeton University Press, 1982), 48-81.

6 See Guido Hoogewoud, Janjaap Kuyt, and Aart Oxenaar, *P. J. H. Cuypers en Amsterdam* ('s-Gravenhage: Staatsuitgeverij, 1985), 80.

7 Alfred Lichtwark, "Museumsbauten," in *Alfred Lichtwark, Eine Auswahl seiner Schriften* (Berlin: Bruno Cassirer, 1917), 178-179.

8 Pieter Singelenberg credits another theoretician of modern museology, B. I. Gilman, as a major source for the design of this museum, but both Berlage and the museum's director, H. E. van Gelder, must have been familiar with Lichtwark's work. See "Het Haags Gemeentemuseum," of "H. P. Berlage, 1856-1934, Een Bouwmeester en zijn Tijd," in *Nederlands Kunsthistorisch Jaarboek*, vol. 25 (Bussum: Fibula Van Dishoeck, 1975):1-89.

9 The museum's original configuration is hard to recognize in the current building, which has been expanded several times.

Towards a New Museum

The following interview was conducted on November 3, 1998, by **Selma Holo**, Director of the USC Fisher Gallery; with **Victoria Newhouse**, author of *Towards A New Museum*, published by Monacelli Press in 1998; **R. Doss Mabe**, partner in Zimmer, Gunsul, Frasca, the architectural firm responsible for designing the highly acclaimed California Science Center at Exposition Park; and **Michael Palladino**, partner, Richard Meier & Partners, responsible for the design of the new Getty Center in Brentwood. The interview was aired on "The Politics of Culture" program, which is produced by KCRW (Los Angeles' National Public Radio station, 89.9 FM).

Selma Holo: Good afternoon. I'm looking forward to talking with the three of you today, about the increasingly visible role of museums in defining the civic lives of our communities. This is a widespread phenomenon and we have seen its manifestations firsthand in Los Angeles. Certainly, our city seems to be holding its collective head significantly higher after the arrival of the Science Center across the street from the University of Southern California, and the Getty Center, near UCLA. But we have also witnessed it in Europe with the virtual rebirthing of a city in Spain's Basque Country. Bilbao, a city most people hadn't even heard of until a few years ago, is now with the advent of its new Guggenheim on everyone's lips, and in everyone's travel plans. I hope we will be able to probe, discuss, and even debate what the role of our new and renewed museums is, and should be, today and in the next century. Certainly in our own city of Los Angeles we are witnesses to strong differences of opinion, which I for one think are signs of our cultural vitality. And so, Victoria, I would like to begin with you, because you have just written a book on the phenomenon of the new museum as related to its architecture. Please tell us what you were trying to describe in that book.

Victoria Newhouse: What I was trying to do, Selma, in *Towards A New Museum* was to evoke, vividly, how museums have been literally revolutionized. Instead of being hushed, sacred, musty places, they are now boisterous centers of popular entertainment. Food, shops, auditoria are now as important as whatever the museum is offering as an exhibit. And all of this has brought about a new kind of building. My book is only about art museums, so Expo Park is not something that I have visited in its entirety. Although I do know parts of it, I have not seen the new Science Center. I've seen many pictures of it and I've read about it and I'm absolutely delighted for this occasion to learn more about it.

SH: Well, then, let me use this opportunity, Victoria, to introduce Doss Mabe who will give us a brief description of what his firm wanted to accomplish when they were awarded the commission to build the Science Center. Was it just about building another beautiful building, or were there larger goals, dare I say, civic goals?

Doss Mabe: That's a good question, Selma, and thanks for having me on the program. As you know, we had been working for a couple of years, prior to receiving the commission for the Science Center, on a master plan for Exposition Park. We found the park, almost ten years ago, in a state of disrepair and in a sense suffering from the same disease that a lot of the central areas in Los Angeles suffer from. Thus, one of the key questions that was on the table was how to retain the institutions that had been in the park for many years. In fact, at the time we were doing the master plan, the LA County Natural History Museum was even contemplating moving its facilities out of the park entirely. And so, a key issue for us was whether we could revive Exposition Park, once a central focus for Los Angeles County at the turn of the century. I think you know that Exposition Park was a kind of Acropolis on the flats for LA then. But by the time we looked at it in the early 1990s the Science Museum had faded somewhat, the Natural History Museum had faded, and the African American Museum had also faded. The Science Center took on, I think, a very bold attitude at that point: its board, its private supporters, decided that they would stay in the center of the city and that they would undertake a massive fundraising project and really revitalize the Science Center. Of course, now, ten years later, that has happened and I'm pleased to say that the other institutions in the park are following suit. Natural History has an ambitious fundraising program now, on its own, and so does the African American Museum.

SH: Terrific, I think then I was not remiss in talking about the civic goals that you aspire to.

DM: That's right.

SH: Michael Palladino, it's your turn to tell us what the Getty Center, from the perspective of its architecture is all about. Richard Meier himself has said, and I quote: "As architects we must make of museums works of art in order to elicit the visitor's pleasure." But is there in your opinion something else besides or in addition to pleasure at stake—something that affects our shared urban life and its possibilities as encapsulated in your creation up on the hill.

Michael Palladino: I think there are a few issues here. The Getty Center has been an extraordinary draw, since it opened, and it has been a draw, I think, for several reasons. First, there's the exceptional collection of art, which a percentage of the population will come to see no matter where it's located. I think we as architects like to think that the architecture is part of the draw... that the buildings, because of the position that they have in the landscape, and their shape and form, draw people to them out of curiosity. But to be honest, I think the site itself for the Getty Center is a draw. The Getty had a number of options back in 1984 when they selected that position in West LA, but they believed that there was a magic to this elevated and central location in Los Angeles, and that the location itself could actually enhance the museum visitor's experience. The thought was that going to a museum would be more than just visiting a collection of art, that it would be a social place where people meet, sit in the courtyard, have a cappuccino. It was anticipated that of the two or three or four hours that one would spend at the museum, maybe half that time would not involve looking at art at all, but being part of a larger group of people, maybe there for lectures, maybe just to have lunch, or to take in the views. It becomes a social place and a destination for a different group of people.

SH: It is wonderful to think of a site as inspiring magic, and I hope we get back to that as we continue the conversation. Now, Victoria, you divide your book into such chapters as the "Museum as Updated Cabinet of Curiosities," the "Museum As Sacred Space," the "Museum As Subject Matter," and, as we've said before, the "Museum as Entertainment." I was surprised that there was no chapter specifically dedicated to the Museum as Civic Space—that type of space destined to enhance the quality of the encounters between visitors, that might contribute to raising the level of human relations in an urban setting, especially one as diverse and complex as Los Angeles. Could you give us some opinions on that, please, and talk a little bit about your organization of the book.

VN: Well, a civic space is something that all of the best museums today achieve. Now, in reading the press about the Getty and Expo Park, there seems to be a tendency to contrast the "high art" Getty and the "low art" Expo Park. But, from what I know about Expo Park, I don't think that this is an accurate contrast. I don't think that they're that different. The Getty, of course, has high art, some great Old Master art, but it's in a setting that in the book I describe as a theme park, and I mean this in the best possible sense. I think that it's an absolutely wonderful format for Southern California: a place where people come to by car or by public transportation and then they take a tram, just the way you would in a theme park, and then they find themselves in this Shangri-La, where they're absolutely forced to go outside, even if it's in covered, glassed-in corridors, but where they can also actually be outside in the open air when they go from one part of the museum to another. This is just like a theme park, where you go from one pavilion to another. And, in between, there are the cappuccino carts, the views, the bookstores—and it's an atmosphere which is all about fun, and excitement. Even though the Getty doesn't have a high-wire bicycle, which I understand there is at the Science Center, it's about meeting people, seeing people, being seen, and socializing.

SH: Now I think we need to talk about the Getty site a bit more. Because, as Victoria has pointed out, even former cynics about the Getty have been remarking that people are enjoying the plaza concept that they encounter on the hill. Michael, the space your firm built really seems to recall European plazas where people soak up the space and the light and enjoy each other, across class and race lines, in ways that some say are not common in Los Angeles. Is this a real and a new urban experience or is it just another extremely artificial and precious encounter that will not have any repercussions?

MP: I have to say that I've spent much time up there watching the crowds. The numbers of people coming alone says something, because those people are going home and telling two more, who tell two more, and the crowds are actually sustaining themselves. It's not just an opening event. It is almost a year since the Getty opening, and we're finding the same kind of mixed and diverse crowds on weekends.

SH: So you seem to think it's entering, sort of, into the fabric of our lives.

MP: Yes, I hate to use an overused term, but the notion of user-friendly museums has to come up here. We've all been to museums where we loved the pictures and where we could spend hours because we're in love with the art. There's a whole population that loves art, but doesn't necessarily need two hours of it. They need to break that up, and I think Victoria said it very well: if the facility can offer the best of both worlds—a proper environment for the collections of art and an environment for those impromptu exchanges between visitors and staff—then it seems to me that it just makes the experience that much more rich.

SH: Still, I wonder whether this label of "theme park" maybe isn't going to be a phrase that we may want to reconsider. Because it does have negative implications, when, in fact the new museum seems to be a very positive phenomenon.

MP: I think you are right. Actually, though, I don't mind the "theme park" label, but I do think the difference between "theme park" and the wide range of what happens at today's museums is considerable. The museum is still about education and is less about the Disneyland kind of theme park entertainment.

VN: When I say "theme park" I'm really thinking about the physical layout, and the fact that it's an indoor/outdoor experience, which of course, Expo Park is also, and for me, this indoor/outdoor experience is typical of Southern California and very appropriate for Southern California. It makes the Getty, and I imagine the museums in Expo Park, distinctive. You know, so many museums today are alike. I won't name names, but we all know what I am talking about. You're in one, you're in another, and you have no idea where you are; you could be in Europe, you could be in the east of the United States, you could be in the west. I think that the rootedness in the physical setting of a locale is a wonderful thing.

SH: Now, Doss, I wonder how you feel about the idea of a theme park in the context of this discussion?

DM: Selma, I've been in LA 15 years now, I've heard a lot of discussions about LA as not a very civic place, not the kind of environment where people come together and actually mix, and I have found that to be, probably, you know, very untrue. Angelenos really search out places like the Getty, and Exposition Park, and you, Michael, and I could name a dozen other spots (and so could any citizen in this city) where one could experience some special kind of civic life. And so I think that one of the most important things with respect to the theme park analogy is that, yes it opens possibilities, but it also narrows the possibilities. I would hate to think that the kinds of places that we're going to experience in the city in the future would be limited in any sense by the idea that they're all variations (cultural variations, art variations, science variations, whatever) on the theme park analogy. And I wonder, as I'm listening, whether that's a rich enough analogy to really circumscribe all of the kinds of places that are being created. LA is incredibly rich to have both the revitalization of Exposition Park and a totally new place, new destination, like the Getty, happening simultaneously. Few cities can boast that. So, I think we really ought to expand that conversation now, and I'm wondering if the analogy of the theme part is also a little limiting. It implies that people would go in their cars to places, and they would enter into them, and participate in them, in much the same spirit they might go to a Disneyland, or a Citywalk. You see, I happen to feel that the real experiences you have at the Getty, or at Expo Park, or any of these other places that we could talk about, are more diverse than that. Let me try a slightly different approach: there's a consumerist aspect about going to a theme park that I think limits the experience a little bit. I think when I go up to the Getty, or when I go to the Science Center on a day when there are literally thousands and thousands of people from all over Los Angeles, I have a totally different kind of feeling, less consumerist, more civic about really touching the city in a new way, in addition to being there to view great works of art, or ride a high-wire bike, or whatever.

SH: I have to agree with you, Doss, that the theme park analogy does perhaps limit us a little. Now, Victoria, I want to ask you about the Centre Pompidou. It's not by accident that the two institutions that we have on this program are the Getty Center and the Science Center. Both have chosen not to use the word museum in their names. Granted there's a Getty Museum within the Getty Center, but we're talking about the whole center today. Is there something enlivening about the notion of a "center" as invented by the Pompidou and that might be of use in our conversation here?

VN: Yes, there is. What the Pompidou did, and its naming of itself was a part of that achievement, was really to topple art off its pedestal. I mean, the Pompidou, first of all, is not only a museum. In fact, there are more people going to the library in the Centre Pompidou than there are going to the museum. What the Pompidou Cultural Center is attempting to do is to place art on a par with a number of other disciplines. It isn't only a library; it is also a music institute, and design center, a center for film, and so forth. And they certainly have achieved some of their purpose, changing the atmosphere of the museum from something very solemn into something more celebratory. I do think "Center" is a very apt way of describing our new cultural enterprises. I think what is interesting about the Getty is that although the museum is out-numbered in terms of other things going on there—the grants program, the conservation institute, the research—it is the museum that has the great public appeal, that creates the great image for the Center.

SH: We're sort of winding down now, and there's something that I'd like to bring up before we conclude. And that is the relationship of these centers to the city itself, to the urban quality of the city of Los Angeles. Doss, you and I have talked about Los Angeles' intrinsic disorder, and in a way your taste for that disorder. Can you say a few words about your Science Center, and the development of Exposition Park, in relationship to the disorder that Los Angeles might represent to you?

DM: I think it's really interesting how, being educated in the East as an urban designer or architect, you come to LA and you bring some European baggage with you. It probably wasn't really until I'd been in LA for a while that I began to appreciate the kind of messy, vital quality that LA has, and the fact that when you take a place like Exposition Park and the Science Center (or I might argue the Getty Center even though it's on a hill and its relationship to the city is very different) in a city like LA, those places as destination play a very different role than, I think, the Pompidou plays. Certainly, if you go back to the Uffizi and a piazza in an Italian city, our destinations are different simply because of the way people get there. Also, I would hope that the diversity and variety of these kinds of institutions in LA, and the way we push them in terms of their content, increase the diversity of the city itself. What I hope is that we don't end up with a formula, whether it's a theme park or whatever, that would sort of dampen down the richness and the vitality and, in a sense, the inherent messiness of a place like LA. Because I think that's part of what being in LA is all about. And so when I read a line like Kirk Forester's, that this [the Getty Center] will be the first urban experience that you really have in LA (and believe me, I'm very fond of the spaces at the Getty, and I think they work very well) I react to it as characterizing the city, in a kind of Euro-centered, looking backward kind of way. To suggest that the Getty is the first place in LA really urbane is, in a sense, a little short-sighted about the city, and maybe indicates a fundamental misunderstanding of LA. So, I think some of what's been written about the Getty from what I would call a Eurocentric position in criticism is probably a little wide of the mark, and actually doesn't do the Getty a service, in terms of its position in the city as well.

MP: I'll just start by saying I agree completely with Doss' comments, and although the Getty offers that kind of urban experience that we all seek out and love, there are many other places in Los Angeles to find them. And, I'll start with where my office is, here in Westwood Village, which needs a little work. In fact we're starting on that now, helping to revitalize the center of Westwood; over the next year or so you'll see a real change. Westwood Village is a terrific, terrific urban center, and there are similar urban centers in Santa Monica, Old Pasadena, and downtown.

SH: Victoria, we're just about running out of time, can you say a closing word or two about this city that you don't live in, but you seem to love.

VN: I certainly do love it. Well, all I can say is that in the nineteenth century, natural history museums were far more central to the civic life of a community than art museums, whose popularity is something relatively new. I think, looking at the success of the Science Center, that it may be re-introducing an old trend in museums, when the non-art museum may once again really compete with art museums in popularity.

DM: I think that's a great observation, Victoria. We look forward to your next book, broadening, really, the kinds of cultural institutions, museums, science centers, and so forth, and talking more about this revolution that's occurring. Because I think that your book really does point out a lot of salient points, which work not only for art museums and what's unfolding in art museums, but also for what's unfolding in all sorts of cultural facilities.

SH: And as we've all been saying, "centers." Michael, do you want to say a parting word or two?

MP: Thank you for having us.

SH: Oh, you're very kind. I must say, in closing, I sense that we are all in agreement on beginning to see a particularity of place developing as an ingredient of our museums in Los Angeles (which we are now calling "centers" for the purpose of this discussion). Their architecture reminds us that our lifestyle is about living inside and outside in a fashion found in few other great cities in the world. They remind us that we are enhancing a special kind of urban existence that we seem to be inventing for ourselves and for our visitors. Our museums are about transcending the homogenization that museums seem to have fallen into elsewhere. We are extremely lucky to have had such distinguished guests with us today on KCRW and I thank them for joining me in discussion of the Politics of Culture.

Building New Museums from the Ground Up

Susana Bautista

Centro Cultural de Tijuana: A New Cultural Paradigm of the Postmodern Condition

In a convoluted world, such as the one in which we live, one asks oneself, what happens with its inhabitants? After so many promises of a better world upon entering the Industrial Revolution, generation after generation has not been able to fulfill this promise. It is probable to accept that a minority lives better with regard to health and material objects, yet the question is, do they live better with regard to the Spiritual, Social, Cultural?[1]

The Centro Cultural de Tijuana (CECUT) was a project conceived by the government organization FONAPAS (Fondo Nacional para las Actividades Sociales) and its president, Mrs. Carmen Romano de Lopez Portillo, wife of the past president of Mexico, José Lopez Portillo. The northwestern peninsular state of Baja California has a history of political and economic independence due to its geographic isolation, having closer ties to its northern neighbor, the United States, than to central Mexico.[2] Mrs. Portillo believed that a cultural center in Tijuana, the most dynamic city in the state, would serve as the best conduit to bring the history and culture of Mexico from pre-Columbian times to this isolated region. The architecture of CECUT reflects this particular goal by employing vernacular elements commonly recognized in all parts of Mexico—soft, earthy colors, massive walls, and large, open plazas in which to congregate. Because this was to be the most important cultural center in the state, Mrs. Portillo also wanted an architectural element that would become its familiar

Fig. 1 Main plaza, with theater and museum in rear.

Fig. 2 Exterior of La Bola.

symbol. Located at the entrance to the center, the large spheric building housing the planetarium and Omnimax theater became this symbol, commonly referred to as *La Bola* (The Ball). It was critical to the founders of CECUT to create an alluring milieu of familiarity, accessibility, and social interaction in order to fulfill its ultimate mission: cultural unification with Mexico. Once the local community accepted the center as their own, rather than a federal project imposed on them, the center was then able to create educational programming towards this end. Most North American museums already recognize this priority of education; however, the founders and architects of CECUT gave priority to the creation of an engaging social milieu so as to attract and retain a first-time audience. The two architects of CECUT, Pedro Ramírez Vázquez and Manuel Rosen Morrison, reflect the strong leftist inclination of Mexico's socio-political culture in their commitment to the social aspirations of architecture, notably museum architecture, as a response to the postmodern condition.[3]

Mrs. Portillo's particular vision of CECUT and its communal obligations are embodied in the *agora*.[4] In ancient Greece, the *agora*, which still functions as an open market in modern Greece, was the central meeting place for all Athenians—a public place where philosophy was discussed, politics debated, and both men and women engaged in commerce. The *agora* symbolizes the new paradigm of CECUT as a cultural center/museum, whose goal is a dialectical relationship between institution and visitor, past and present, and local and national needs. This dialectical, rather than hierarchical, relationship facilitated the acceptance of Mexican history and culture by the Tijuana/Baja community. Thus, Mrs. Portillo's concept of an *agora* reflects, in addition to its Hellenic origins, an intrinsically Mexican sentiment that places great importance on social needs. CECUT, accordingly, was envisioned as a meeting place for the people of Tijuana—a place to congregate, discuss, read, and learn.[5]

Architecturally, the concept of an *agora* as a social construct is reflected in two international trends that have pervaded Mexico since the early 1900s. The strong functionalist tradition of modern Mexico, inspired by the great French architect Le Corbusier, was expressed by his disciple, Mexican architect and artist Juan O'Gorman, as "the maximum of return with the minimum of effort."[6] This tradition greatly influenced Mexican muralists, artists, and architects alike in the 1920s. However, while the functionalists advanced a strong social sense, they also inhibited the creative imagination of the architect. It was instead the rationalist tradition of the 1960s that held out greater promise of providing a rational architectural response to the country's postrevolutionary social problems. Nevertheless, both ideologies were eagerly embraced by a postcolonial country desperately trying to modernize itself amidst internal strife in the early twentieth century.[7] Ramírez Vázquez and Rosen Morrison were both recipients of this birth of Mexican Modernism. While influenced by such international styles, they were, however, also indebted to a much older patrimony that looks beyond the Spanish Colonial period to the monumental architecture of the Mayans, Aztecs, and other indigenous Indians. A consequence of the merger of all of these influences is a respect for muted, monochromatic earth colors, severe geometric designs, massive flat walls, and stone, sand, and cement materials—in short, for the colors, shapes, and substances of the land (fig. 1). Ruth Rivera, a contemporary Mexican architect, termed this merger *integración plástica* (plastic integration), and Edward Burian, in his book *Modernity and the Architecture of Mexico*, called it both a formal device and an innately Mexican quality.[8] Supported by functionalist and rationalist ideologies, twentieth-century Mexican architecture developed its postcolonial identity by ultimately accepting Mexico's diverse heritage—the indigenous and the European, the local and the national. This identity is realized at CECUT in an architecture that reflects homogenous, national values.

Pedro Ramírez Vázquez, Mexico's foremost architect of the twentieth century, is responsible for building most of its museums, cultural centers, and pavilions, as well as some of those in countries such as the Dominican Republic, Switzerland, Egypt, Nicaragua, and Senegal. He has always been aware of the need for the architectural language of museums to speak on multilateral levels, necessitating the use of colors, shapes, and materials not identified with a specific epoch or region of a country, but rather with its common temporal and spatial history. Three of his early museums—Gallery of History (1960), Museum of Anthropology (1964), and Museum of Modern Art (1964)—are all situated inside Chapultepec Park in Mexico City, a location that facilitates accessibility in a familiar social and public space. At CECUT, Ramírez Vázquez and Rosen Morrison have also achieved this accessibility mainly through two spaces: the prominent spheric building and the large plaza, both situated at the entrance and clearly visible from Tijuana's main boulevards. This creation of a familiar and accessible space was essential if CECUT was to promote local cultural awareness into acceptance of the nation's history and culture.

La Bola, the sphere, has become the familiar symbol of CECUT (fig. 2). This circular building houses an Omnimax movie theater with a 180-degree screen. The building also functions as a planetarium, a theater that seats about 330 people, and a multi-media space for exhibitions on astronomy and physical phenomena (fig. 3). In 1994, CECUT's Omnimax was one of the ten most visited in the world and continues to be extremely popular among the local community, showing three films daily and three premieres annually since 1986.[9] Some of the films that have been shown are: *Chronos, Living Planet, The Grand Canyon, Darwin and the Galapagos, Freedom of Movement, Water and Man, Speed, The First Emperor of China, Niagara Falls, The Blue Planet, Ring of Fire*, and *Tropical Jungle*. The form of the building follows its specific function, as the spheric shape outside simulates the semi-circular screen inside. It was important to Mrs. Portillo and the architects to emphasize the Omnimax theater as the only one in Baja California, as well as playing an integral part in the educational programming of CECUT. In stark contrast to the two-dimensional flatness of the massive exterior walls of the center, *La Bola* soon became the recognizable symbol for both CECUT and the city of Tijuana.

Fig. 3 Ground floor, used as exhibition space.

Fig. 4 Museum entrance from the main plaza.

The second element of CECUT that addresses function and accessibility is the large, open plaza at the entrance (fig. 4). Located on the corner of one of the main boulevards in Tijuana, the central plaza measures approximately twelve thousand square feet. The use of large plazas and courtyards can be traced to Spanish Colonial architecture from the sixteenth century, but the basic concept of an open public space was equally essential to the much earlier pre-Columbian society. Today, the plaza is the center around which religious, commercial, and social life revolves in every village and city in Mexico. CECUT's plaza is as functional as its predecessors, with live performances of music and dance, activities for children, and celebrations of national festivities, all intended to promote participation and interaction. In its dual function as the main entrance to the center and as a familiar meeting place for all Mexicans, the plaza thus encourages accessibility to the rest of CECUT.

Fig. 5 Main staircase of the museum.

Familiarity and accessibility were important criteria for CECUT, because of the state of Baja California's disjunctive relationship with central Mexico—geographically, economically, politically, and historically. At first, Tijuana resented that CECUT was a federal rather than a local project, and during its early years the center was poorly attended and supported by the local community. Whether or not the architects and founders foresaw this initial rejection, the architecture contributed to the acceptance of CECUT by responding to the basic social needs of Tijuana, a postmodern, progressive city lacking in a sense of history or a cohesive relationship with either the United States or Mexico, and consequently also in a national identity. Within these conditions, CECUT has been working for eighteen years to find the paradigmatic antidote based on its architecture and programming. The architecture is presented in a vernacular language understood by Mexicans with a nostalgia for their common history. Alberto Pérez-Gómez, Mexican architect and author of *Architecture and the Crisis of Modern Science*, refers to this process of understanding as "a deep sense of recognition."[10] The natural earth colors, the imposing walls derived from pre-Columbian civic and religious architecture, the large plaza, the spheric building that has been compared to the Mayan Ball game—all remind the citizens of Baja peninsula of their national heritage and bring them closer to central Mexico.

In order to first attract the Tijuana community, however, the center's curatorial and educational programming was committed to primarily local concerns. This parochial attention has played a major part in the transformation of Tijuana's image from "Tijuana the Sinner, Tijuana the Pervert" to "Tijuana the Refuge for Everyone," as described in a recent *Los Angeles Times* article entitled "Mexico's City of Promise."[11] The focus on local educational programming, coupled with the inclusion of architectural elements that reflect Mexico's rich heritage, enabled CECUT to achieve its goal of unifying regional and national aspirations.

Since its inception in 1982, the founders and directors of CECUT have regarded education as their priority. In 1994, the importance of education was affirmed in its official publication, *Centro Cultural Tijuana en el Centro de la Cultura*: "Now [CECUT] has before it the possibility of converting itself into a true center of artistic education, that we would all like to see renovated and strengthened in the entire country."[12] Educational programs include temporary visual art exhibitions of artists and architects from Baja California, central Mexico, and Latin America; a permanent collection of regional archaeological artifacts; local, national, and international theater performances with the Orchestra of Baja California in residence; a bilingual library and bookstore; a planetarium; and classes teaching the visual and performing arts (fig. 5). CECUT is especially proud of its *Programa de Promoción Escolar* (Program for Scholastic Promotion), initiated in 1983, that transports approximately a thousand children daily from the state, municipal, and federal school systems to the center. The main plaza is used for many of these activities, such as performing folkloric dances, teaching arts and crafts, and celebrating national festivities (fig. 6). In 1988, the center also published a museum didactic guide designed for educators within these school systems. This program operates in conjunction with the Secretary of Public Education and the National Council on the Arts and Culture and has remained a priority for the center.

In their original plans of 1980, Ramírez Vázquez and Rosen Morrison included a third floor above the administrative and commercial areas to house the visual and performing arts classes pivotal to CECUT's educational component. Due to both budgetary restraints and an initial lack of local interest, this space was never completed. Instead, these classes have taken place in make-shift spaces at the center over the last ten years. As CECUT has been gradually embraced by Tijuana and Baja California, the demand has grown for classes in the dramatic arts, guitar and music, scenography, painting, and many other

Fig. 6 Activities for the public in the main plaza.

visual and performing arts. Today, the architects are once again discussing with the federal government the possibility of building that third floor for adequate classroom space, but now the hindrance is solely economic.[13]

While most North American museums acknowledge education as a top priority, they differ with CECUT in how to realize that goal. In response to a decrease in funding for the arts, these museums have started to offer services such as quality restaurants and cafes, computer interactive exhibitions and websites, and film and live performances to attract visitors. CECUT, despite the advantage of federal support—although it is not always reliable because of shifting political parties or economic instability—must also confront demanding local constituencies and public opinion. Mrs. Portillo's answer to these civic needs was the *agora.* Materialized architecturally as the guiding principle of CECUT, the *agora* symbolizes a society concerned with a high level of social, cultural, and economic interchange. CECUT's *agora* incorporates the spheric building within the plaza, reinforcing the inclusion of social activities in the architectural space of the plaza. Whereas *La Bola* clearly attracts visitors by its conspicuous shape and its connection to popular cinema, the plaza greets visitors with a timeless language of familiarity and history that appeals to a predominately local audience. Through these means CECUT attracts visitors to its unknown and potentially intimidating cultural spaces. As a response to the postmodern condition of isolation, Ramírez Vázquez and Rosen Morrison have consolidated Mexico's past and present with Mexico's socialist inclinations into timeless architectural elements. As Ramírez Vázquez explains:

> *Architecture should be at the service of others, not of the author; I have, therefore, never been concerned about making an architecture that will be identified with me, but with the service it should give the direct user, within or without, enriching the environment and contributing to the artistic heritage.*[14]

As art museums in North America, both private and public, approach the twenty-first century they have become more culturally and socially aware than their nineteenth-century predecessors, an awareness reflected in a shift of focus from the interests of the few to those of the community. They are also more responsive to the general public's expectation of service, technological support, and entertainment. Curatorial and educational programs have begun including ethnographical and historical artifacts, in addition to works of art, in exhibitions. On the West Coast, such contextual expansion of educational offering is occurring in the Armand Hammer Museum of Art and Cultural Center, the Skirball Cultural Center and Museum, UCLA Fowler Museum of Cultural History, the Latino Museum of History, Art and Culture, and the Bowers Museum of Cultural History in Santa Ana. This trend can also be observed on the East Coast in the Solomon R. Guggenheim Museum. Known for its important collection of modern art, the Guggenheim has organized two controversial exhibitions since 1997: *The Art of the Motorcycle* and *China: 5,000 Years.* As society continues to endure the postmodern condition, museums must respond appropriately in programming and architecture. Educational programs of the twenty-first century can teach people how to integrate within their increasingly heterogeneous communities and how to search for the homogeneous. Museum architecture must support this critical social end. Ramírez Vázquez describes the ideal museum as "an objective and permanent educational building, [which] must be easily understood by people of all cultural levels, a place where visitors will behold the objects it contains, will learn and be proud of the past, and help them to be useful in the future."[15] The educational programs of CECUT have fostered re-education of Tijuana's citizenry to think of themselves as part of the larger context of Mexican history, and thus has encouraged a closer identification of the state of Baja California with the larger geographical unit of Mexico.

1 Manuel Rosen Morrison, personal unpublished notes translated by author, on "Cultural Centers or *Agoras*," La Jolla, CA, April 1998.

2 Anne-Marie O'Connor, "Maquiladora Women Finding Freedom," *Los Angeles Times*, 27 January 1998, A8. With high unemployment, Baja California and the rest of the northern border states of Mexico are economically dependent on the United States for jobs. Maquiladoras, or foreign factories, entered Mexico during the 1960s to employ those who found themselves without a job after the demise of the twenty-year federal bracero program that brought Mexicans across the border into the United States for temporary work. Although some factories are from Asia, the majority continue to be from the United States. Mexico now has one million maquiladora workers, mostly along the border states in northern Mexico, and one in three working women in Baja work in the maquiladoras.

3 I am not using the term postmodern in the architectural sense, which explains the spelling as "postmodern" and not as "Post-Modern." Nor am I using the term according to literary theory, but rather as articulated by the cultural theorist Homi Bhabha. I have found Bhabha's writings very useful for this analysis of CECUT and modern Mexican architecture because of his attempt to "rename the postmodern from the position of the postcolonial." (Homi Bhabha, *The Location of Culture* [London: Routledge Press, 1994], 175.) The search for the location of culture, both temporally and spatially, is of primary concern to the postcolonial society in its search for an independent, modern identity within a larger historical discourse. CECUT represents Mexico's, and particularly Tijuana's, search for culture and identity in a postmodern society still determined by its postcolonial perspective.

4 Manuel Rosen Morrison, interview by author, tape recording, La Jolla, CA, 13 February 1998. It was most interesting that Mr. Rosen interchangeably referred to CECUT as the *agora* during our conversation.

5 Rosen Morrison compares the cultural center to a modern *agora*, or supermarket. Shopping used to be a social event in Mexico, as it was in the ancient Greek *agora*. Today, shopping is an isolated activity, and the modern supermarket an "inhospitable space without bargaining, without interaction, and without enjoyment; [shopping] is dehumanized." (Rosen Morrison interview.) As my argument will demonstrate, Rosen Morrison tried architecturally to revive this humanizing aspect of the pre-Columbian market in the contemporary *agora* of CECUT.

6 I. E. Myers, *Mexico's Modern Architecture* (New York: Architectural Book Publishing Co., 1952), 11.

7 Mexico's postrevolutionary social problems stem from the 1910-1917 revolution that brought an end to the Porfiriato, the dictatorship of Porfírio Díaz. The Mexican revolution was a final cry for democracy and social justice, a revolt by the common people against landowners, mining and industrial capitalists, and the dictatorship. The origins of these social problems, however, can be traced to Mexico's postcolonial period that began in 1821 with the end of three hundred years of Spanish dominion in Mexico. It was during this period that Mexico began its tumultuous search for a national identity, a search fraught with civil and political strife, economic disparities, and social inequalities between indigenous Indians and Spanish descendants.

8 Edward R. Burian, ed., *Modernity and the Architecture of Mexico* (Austin: University of Texas Press, 1997), 29.

9 Consejo Nacional para la Cultura y las Artes, *Centro Cultural Tijuana en el Centro de la Cultura* (Tijuana, Mexico: Consejo Nacional para la Cultura y las Artes, 1994), 2.

10 Burian, 41.

11 Anne-Marie O'Connor, "Mexico's City of Promise," *Los Angeles Times*, 26 January 1998, A1.

12 Consejo Nacional para la Cultura y las Artes, 2.

13 Pedro Ramírez Vázquez was able to understand and interpret the intentions of Mrs. Portillo because of his experience with scholastic architecture. He was chief architect responsible for the construction of prefabricated rural classrooms throughout Mexico from 1958 to 1989. Responding to a serious need for primary education in the rural areas of Mexico lacking in roads and funds, he thus provided a simple and economical solution to the problem. Ramírez Vázquez won the Grand Prize of Honor at the XII Triennial of Milan in 1960 for these classrooms and schools, which have since been adopted in over twenty Latin American countries as well as in India, Indonesia, Yugoslavia, and Italy.

14 Javier Pizarro, ed., *Ramírez Vázquez* (Mexico City: García Valades Editores, 1989), 215.

15 Ann Lee Morgan and Colin Naylor, eds., *Contemporary Architects* (Chicago: St. James Press, 1987), 729.

Ariadni Ariane Liokatis

The Museum of Contemporary Art, Los Angeles: Singular Art Centerpiece of the Bunker Hill Cultural Corridor?

The Museum of Contemporary Art (MOCA) sits amidst a fleet of skyscrapers (fig. 1) at the heart of downtown Los Angeles, the city's financial and economic headquarters. While MOCA constitutes the only art museum in this area, other culturally allied institutions are located nearby in what can soon be thought of as a vital arts corridor: the Music Center, the Los Angeles Central Public Library, the Colburn School of Performing Arts, the soon-to-be completed Disney Hall, and, as well, the Cathedral of Angels. This ensemble of facilities will quicken the cultural vitality of downtown, and attract a larger public to an area whose revitalization the city has been working to realize for the past twenty years or so.

Since its origin in the Olvera Street area, downtown has only fitfully and nominally constituted the heart of metropolitan Los Angeles, the sum of a vast number of eclectic parts incorporating eighty-eight separate municipalities within its boundaries. As a result, Los Angeles, a sprawling and fragmented megalopolis, has for much of this century lacked a geographical center and recognizable landmarks—other than the freeway system, itself a sign of its ubiquitous sprawl. The enthusiasm for urban renewal, however, has prompted the city's authorities to try forging a definite vital core for the City of Angels in the shape of a real downtown with its center in the Bunker Hill district.

Fig. 1 The Museum of Contemporary Art, Los Angeles, set against a backdrop of skyscrapers.

MOCA was conceived in the context of this downtown urban rejuvenation. An innovative reinterpretation of public art funding enabled the museum's incorporation into the California Plaza scheme, a redevelopment project aimed at the rehabilitation of the historic but, since the end of World War II, mostly derelict area of Bunker Hill overlooking the rest of downtown. This scheme, launched in the early eighties, projected a complex of offices, residential towers, shops, and restaurants, as well as a hotel. The condominiums and rental units were intended to induce people to live in the area, and the entire complex was meant to become a focus for downtown, a social centerpiece where people live, work, shop, dine, and encounter culture and art. MOCA, as the sole art museum in this plan, was regarded by California Plaza developers, city hall, and Mayor Tom Bradley as a key element of the ambitious project that would metamorphose downtown into a meaningful urban core. The subtext was that Los Angeles would then assume its rightful authority as America's capital of the Pacific Rim. In this scheme of things, it was believed that "A major art museum in downtown Los Angeles would help solve the dilemma of how to transmogrify an agglomeration of high-rises into a city with a meaningful core."[1] MOCA's birth thus shares in, and contributes to, the museum resurgence that has been taking place in this last quarter of the century: no longer mere transparent and neutral shelters for the preservation and display of works of art, museums have become "barometers of an urban, and in some cases, of a national cultural virility.... These museums are the kings, queens and sometimes aces in each city's hand as they vie with each other across the Western world for attention."[2] While the completion of this ambitious urban renovation is still years in the future, MOCA constitutes an integral component of the music, theater, and opera mix being developed on Bunker Hill. The social-urban mandate envisioned by those who financed the museum remains an ambitious one for a young institution; nevertheless, the verdict on the ultimate success of its contribution to the civic renewal of the area, while still out, bodes well, given its singular position in the cultural life of downtown Los Angeles.

Fig. 2 Aerial view of MOCA.

If architectural distinction alone can produce the miracle of establishing an attractive cynosure in an otherwise architecturally undistinguished area, then MOCA has won half the battle. At least, architects and critics of architecture would have us believe it to be so. In her recent book, *Towards a New Museum*, on the development of museum architecture in the late-twentieth century, Victoria Newhouse stresses that "the success or failure of these new museums, in aesthetic, educational and financial terms, results from a variety of factors, none more important than their architecture."[3] Architecturally speaking, MOCA is a relatively small-sized and low-rise museum (due to height and massing restrictions imposed by the developers), which manages an elegant, however diminutive, profile besides California Plaza's crass high-rises. MOCA is indeed often called a gem, a jewel in a forest of skyscrapers. Arata Isozaki, its Japanese architect, created

Fig. 3 Access to the museum from the east through the sculpture court; barrel-vaulted library and boardroom on left; office block and bookstore on right.

an exquisite and highly-finished structure, which has been consistently elected, since its completion in 1986, as one of America's ten best museum buildings (fig. 2). Given the greatly constrained and limited physical possibilities for design of the museum, the architect managed to devise an eminently workable solution for this particular site. The building is divided into two distinct entities featuring the formal power of Isozaki's signature assemblage of geometric forms: cylinder, cube, and pyramid. The museum's barrel-vaulted library (fig. 3) and the pyramidal skylights constitute MOCA's dominant visual outline and determine the building's distinctive character. Isozaki also intentionally introduced tones not commonly encountered among the bright colors and stucco of Los Angeles's architectural landscape in order to distinguish his edifice and make it stand out. The use of red Indian sandstone (both cleft- and honed-finished), dark green aluminum panels, and copper-sheathing—all unusual for the region—produces an interaction between contrasting textures and colors, which adds rich density to the geometric outline of the museum structures. Finally, envisioning the museum as a "village in a valley of skyscrapers," Isozaki fractioned the building mass to enable it to compete visually with the surrounding high-rises,

Fig. 4 The Centre Georges Pompidou, Paris.

believing that "this fragmented assembly would have a symbolic effect on the oppressive inhumanity of the immense high-rise buildings in the vicinity and would offer pedestrian visitors to the museum an intermediate scale space."[4]

Isozaki's building and architectural design has succeeded in giving MOCA a distinctive personality and helped position the institution nationally and internationally as a contemporary art collecting center. However, MOCA is hemmed in by the tall buildings, and its diminutive profile undermines claims to urban monumentality. As the Centre Pompidou—which became a national monument—has shown, however, size does indeed matter. It might be informative to compare MOCA with the Beaubourg, as the Centre Pompidou is popularly known by its site, whose goals and urban mandate were not unlike those of the local museum's. Inaugurated in 1977, the Centre Pompidou (fig. 4) was intended to revivify the wholesale food market area in the center of Paris, and to endow the city with a leading cultural center, which would reposition France as a leader in the world of artistic creativity. Designed by Renzo Piano and Richard Rogers, who transformed the initial concept of a cultural center into a live center of culture, information, and entertainment, as they termed it, the Centre Pompidou is a monumental and highly flexible mixed-use cultural institution that comprises the Museum of Modern Art, a library, an institute of research in music and acoustics, an industrial design center, an auditorium, a restaurant, and a bar. The building's iconoclastic and controversial architecture—a five-story glass-walled skeleton of steel with servicing ducts and pipes a visible component of the external fabric of the structure—provoked a revolution in museum design. The Centre Pompidou called for the desacralization of art and launched the concept of the museum as entertainment. It has proven a successful catalyst for an urban and cultural resurgence. A measure of its popular success is its annual attendance of eight million visitors. Its central location and the efficient Parisian public transportation network make it a highly accessible site. The active popular life of the former wholesale market district is reproduced by the Centre Pompidou's outdoor plaza, a privileged site for social interaction, where a variety of street performances take place. Many visit the institution to ogle this ever-changing street scene, and to ride on the escalators up the side of the glass façade for a view of Paris and its architectural landmarks.

Although MOCA has helped put Los Angeles on the cultural map, the museum's populist appeal is hampered by its inaccessibility and its relatively small size, which cannot accommodate large numbers of visitors, such as those pouring into the Beaubourg. Los Angeles's poor public transportation network, limited street parking, and expensive public garage charges, as well as the confusing street pattern in the vicinity of MOCA, are important deterrents to many. In addition, the rich street life of the Latino shopping blocks of Broadway is too distant to encounter on Bunker Hill. In contrast, the Centre Pompidou easily accomodates the overflow of people from the gigantic shopping attraction Forum of Chatelet Halles.

Fig. 5 Entrance to galleries, viewed from lobby.

In comparison to the Centre Pompidou, which epitomizes the notion of the museum as entertainment and is often referred to as the palace of fun with its architecture borrowing the playfulness of theme parks, MOCA can be said to conform to the traditional conception of the museum as a temple of art. Isozaki has created a highly-finished edifice for this museum, and a precious container for the art. The warm intimacy of MOCA's interior—with its natural light from triangular skylights, flexibility of movable walls allowing easy expansion and contraction of exhibition areas, and straightforward layout of rooms—offers attractive working and viewing possibilities for the temporary exhibitions and for the permanent collection (fig. 5 and 6). In its treatment of space, MOCA realizes an easy triumph over the Centre Pompidou's cavernous ground floor environs and balcony terraces, not to mention the tortuous mazes of its fourth and fifth floor temporary and permanent galleries.

MOCA's diminutive elegance is also far removed from the "self-effacing warehouse" that the museum's initial representatives envisioned and desired. In the first stages of MOCA's construction, the institution was represented by an architecture committee who conceived the museum primarily as an active forum for the generation and exchange of artistic ideas, and whose architectural conception for the facility was a plain warehouse-like façade, resembling industrial spaces and artists' lofts—an "ideal, quintessential, contemporary artist space... [conveying] the message that the art inside would be art-in-process."[5] This design implied minimal disturbance from an architecture privileged over the art and boasting an architect's forceful signature. Eventually, Isozaki's belief that the building's architecture had a significant symbolic role to play for both the city and the arts prevailed over the anonymous structure.

Indeed, a warehouse would not have served the museum's symbolic status as part of the downtown arts corridor. Fortuitously, MOCA's other building, the Geffen Contemporary, constitutes the warehouse that the museum's initial representatives, composed in major part of artists, wished for. This highly flexible and multi-disciplinary pair of industrial warehouses, renovated by Frank Gehry in 1983, has proven very popular with artists, because the space resembles many artists' studios, embodies their vitality, and encourages the experimental. While it may appear that Southern California artists are primarily exhibited at the Geffen rather than at the California Plaza facility, both venues practice a balanced display of local, national. and international, established and emergent artists. With this said, it must be acknowledged that the general public finds the Geffen more accessible and probably feels more at ease in its spaces than those at the California Plaza. While the Centre Pompidou called for the democratization of both art and the museum and introduced an array of social attractions in the traditionally sacred museum space to make art more accessible and to bring in a larger public, MOCA has performed a balancing act of satisfying both the high and the low, the elitist and the democratic demands of a late twentieth-century art museum simultaneously belonging to the patron and to the people.

Fig. 6 Gallery.

MOCA has acquired the stature of a cultural landmark in downtown Los Angeles. Its architecture befits its placement at the center of the cultural corridor running from the massive Music Center anchoring the north end to the graceful Los Angeles Central Public Library adorning the south end. In this schematic recreation of Bunker Hill as the artistic adornment of downtown Los Angeles, MOCA more than holds its own vis-à-vis the other contributing institutions.

1 Jo-Anne Berelowitz, "The Museum of Contemporary Art, Los Angeles: An Account of Collaboration between Artists, Trustees and an Architect," in *Art Apart: Art Institutions and Ideology Across England and North America*, ed. Marcia Pointon (Manchester, New York: Manchester University Press, 1994), 268-269.

2 Ian Ritchie, "The Museum as Public Architecture," in *Museum Builders*, ed. James Steele (London: Academy Editions, 1994), 10.

3 Victoria Newhouse, inside jacket of *Towards a New Museum* (New York: The Monacelli Press, 1998).

4 Arata Isozaki, "A Chain of Subtle Changes," *The Japan Architect*, 358 (February 1987): 22-23.

5 Berelowitz, 277.

Susan M. Kahn

The Seattle Art Museum: A Post-Modernist Architecture of Ironic Self-Denial

The new site for the Seattle Art Museum had already been acquired when the architect was selected in 1988, but a more appropriate site is hard to imagine for honky-tonk populist[1] Robert Venturi, whose firm, Venturi, Scott Brown and Associates (VSBA), was then refining a building type described as "the popular art museum in the center of town."[2] Seemingly a perfect fit for Venturi's architectural ideas, the Seattle museum was to be located between First and Second Avenues on University Street in a section of downtown Seattle described by a museum official as one step from skid row, adjacent to pawn shops, tattoo parlors, and adult movie houses, such as the Lusty Lady.

Originally founded by the Fuller family and located in lovely, turn-of-the-century Volunteer Park, the museum's selection of a downtown site for its new building must be viewed as a democratic gesture—intended to accommodate a broader collection and to reach a more diverse audience. The impulse is indicative of the radical changes that museums have undergone since the last century. No longer a hushed space in which gentlemen in top hats accompanied by ladies with parasols contemplate aesthetics, museums today are crowded with thousands of people from different "taste cultures," there not only to view art, but also to learn, and to be entertained. Three-fourths of the floor space at the new museum was earmarked for non-gallery space, including restaurant, museum shop, auditorium, and education facilities. The architect's mission, then, was to reconcile the former grandeur of the institution with the new demographics and performance requirements, *i.e.*, to create an American museum with both popular appeal and a sense of permanence.

Fig. 1 Detail of ornamental pediment.

To the art collectors comprising the board of directors, Bob Venturi was their man.[3] The architect first found acclaim in 1966 with the publication of *Complexity and Contradiction in Architecture*,[4] in which he shunned the prevailing model of the spare office monolith in favor of a more eclectic style. In *Learning from Las Vegas* (1972),[5] he and his coauthors made the case for understanding and appreciating

Fig. 2 Exterior of Seattle Art Museum, seen from First Avenue.

commercial sprawl. Better, they asserted, casino architecture with its blaring neon signs—"decorated sheds"—than "ducks," buildings that attempt to convey their purpose through tortured structural symbolism. Cited as the father of Post-Modernism, Venturi's approach incorporated historical references and imagery from popular culture into contemporary buildings.

Given carte blanche in the Seattle project, VSBA created a complex structure intended to appeal to a broad audience by the use of such stratagems as symbolic ornament and architectural contradiction. The architects' use of ornament animates the exterior façade where historical references playfully abound—nor is it necessary to understand the allusions to be taken by their charm. However, the visitor is alternately beckoned and repelled by contradictory elements of the interior space, such as the "damned pillar on the other side of the front door."[6] Ironically, VSBA's "urban art museum" resists popular access as much as its predecessor in Volunteer Park.

Any analysis of the Seattle Art Museum (SAM) inevitably begins with its exterior, where formal and informal elements are juxtaposed (fig. 2). As a city of dualities in which runners rub shoulders with businessmen in Seattle's lively center, the happy consequence is that locals find the museum alluring. The building conveys a stature that transcends its diminutive size—a stature attributable, in part, to the incised name of the place that functions as a cornice, to Jonathan Borofsky's towering Hammering Man at the entrance, and to the elegant grand stairway commanding the interior and visible from the exterior. Yet, with vivacious modesty, in keeping with the city's demeanor, the museum eschews a serious mien in favor of balancing its architectural historicity with popular elements. For example, High Art/Imperial Rome is countered by Pop Art/Las Vegas in the museum's signage. The fourteen-foot-high letters of the institution's name wrap around two elevations, announcing the museum's presence to the city at large. Roman lettering suggests the institution's privileged past, as does the fluting of the surrounding limestone. As a counterpoint, since roof-level cornices, however Beaux Arts grand, are not ordinarily noticed at street level, the second sign over the entrance arch is unmistakable to pedestrians. Much smaller, its plain black letters are wittily encased by the "bubble lights" of a movie theater marquee.

In theory at least, the symbolism of the façade ornamentation provides a metaphorical point of entry for the general public. According to Venturi, symbolism can "provide a diversity of architectural vocabularies appropriate for a plurality of tastes and sensitive to qualities of heritage and place. This use suits the need to respond in our time to

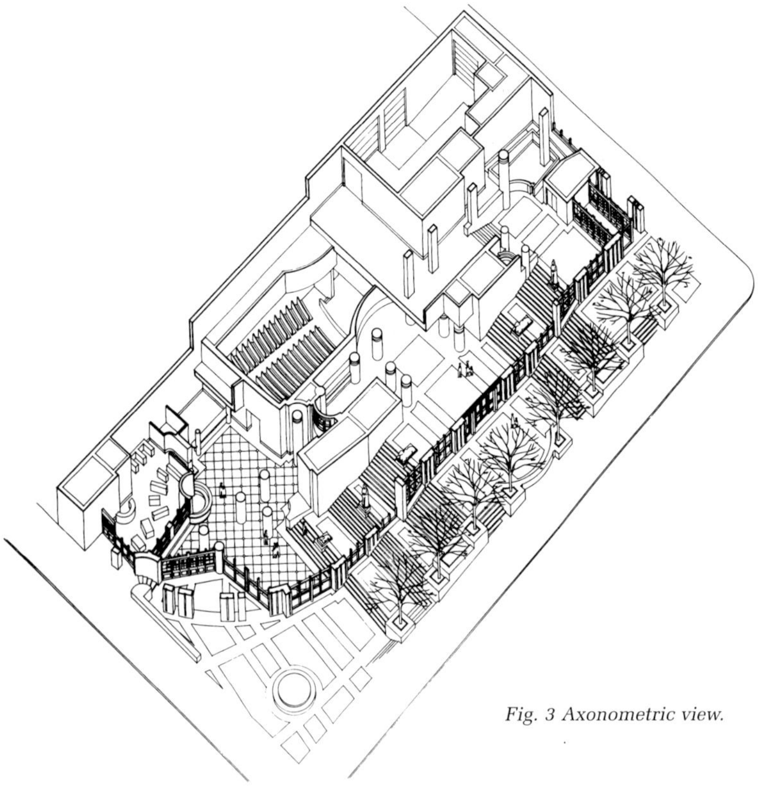

Fig. 3 Axonometric view.

both mass culture and pluralist expression."[7] SAM's colorful, running pediment of painted tiles serves as a mannered site for myriad historical references: Egyptian lotus flowers and brightly-colored acantha capitals, Babylonian glazed tiles, Romanesque round arches, Gothic flying buttresses and pointed arches, and Islamic ogee arches (fig. 1). While these citations recall monumental civic buildings through history, they do not relate specifically to Seattle—notwithstanding one critic's tenuous assertion that the whole serves as a metaphor for a city where difference is appreciated and elements are reconciled, not integrated.[8]

Indeed, there is little contextualization involved in VSBA's project for Seattle, other than its conformation to the topography of the site.[9] Instead, the boxy structure with one rounded corner embodies the architects' generic "decorated shed," defined as "systems of space and structure [that] are directly at the service of program, and [where] ornament is applied independently of them."[10] The careers of Venturi and his wife and partner, Denise Scott Brown, began at the advent of Pop Art, the movement marking the end of Modernism and heralding a new era of commodification. Accordingly, a building, like any other product, is an object of consumption. No longer contextualized, it is set apart, its contents contained by a wrapper.[11] Plain and utilitarian in shape, ornament is applied to its surface—ornament whose primary function is communication via symbolism.

The problem is that the message of SAM's ornamentation is intended for an elite audience and this is especially evident where its Post-Modernist architects joke about Modernism. Ornament articulating the exterior walls slyly indicates the internal arrangement of the structure (fig. 2). Overall, the form of the building does not follow function, yet ironically the ornamentation of the tripartite division of the exterior does. At the very top of the building is a curtain wall. Typical of adjacent office buildings, this glazed surface identifies the location of SAM's administrative offices. In the middle is a limestone façade; windowless like an armory, it designates the repository of the museum's "treasure," its art. Lastly, the lively, decorative area at street level marks the area devoted to people and services: entrance, museum store, auditorium, education rooms, and atrium leading to the grand stair. More subtle is the architects' metaphor for Modernism's "curtain wall." The south elevation, manifestly a curtain wall by virtue of its glazed base, looks like fabric. The vertical striations are the pleats of a skirt, the ornamental pediment that dances across the façade its embroidered hem. If the untutored visitor does not get the joke, he or she can nonetheless appreciate the rather klutzy box, which exudes bonhomie. "We want it to be pretty," Venturi said, and to appeal to children.[12] SAM does cheer a misty Seattle day. The polychromy of its dancing pediment appeals to all, even if the precise architectural allusions are only appreciated by the erudite few.

Regrettably, SAM's cheerful exterior is blown by VSBA's heavy-handed imposition of architectural theory in the interior design—theory that nearly thwarts the visitor, scholar and layman alike. The problems begin at the entrance, or, more precisely, at the entrances, for there are two. Entry through the Second Avenue door (at the top of the site and facing the city) is the more efficient way to the galleries, which are housed on the second through fourth floors. However, the impact of the grand stair is compromised when viewed from above, because the Chinese tomb sculptures that line the stairs are backwards, facing downward. More troubling is the $50,000 a year it costs to maintain the Second Avenue entrance. Using the noise and dirt from construction of Symphony Hall across the street as an excuse, the museum closed this door "temporarily," reducing costs and actually increasing revenue by converting the coat check area into a special exhibit store.

Once the more decorous entry on First Avenue (at the bottom of the site and facing Puget Sound) is determined, visitors encounter two prosaic sets of doors: one friendly, the other inimical. On the one hand, there are the warm, friendly "school doors," made of humble oak with paned windows, and on the other, the tortuously-accessed revolving door. Grudgingly complying with energy conservation requirements, VSBA tucked the "spin-around" door into an obscure corner and made it dark and narrow. Visitors resist using this door—which is unfortunate, because, according to Senior Deputy Director Gail Joice, "It could have helped direct the flow of traffic inside the museum."[13]

Notwithstanding Venturi's awareness of the potential for visitor confusion in the foyer of a museum, where the tangle of service areas can seem to make the art remote, even beyond reach,[14] that bewilderment prevailed initially at SAM. Local architects were called in shortly after the museum opened to make this space less confusing (fig. 3). They could not, however, do anything about the huge weight-bearing column in the midst of the foyer space, which obstructs direct passage to the grand stair and the art beyond (fig. 4). Even with models, museum officials "didn't see this coming."[15] VSBA, however, intentionally planned it as a challenge to the visitor's entry into the museum. Leaving aside the value of such a challenge, the device is a roadblock. "Try to get the school groups around [the column]...that [stratagem] doesn't work for us," Joice flatly states.[16]

Once out of the low-ceilinged foyer and past the columnar sentry, the visitor enters the vast, dramatic space of the grand stairway, punctuated at intervals with immense Chinese tomb sculptures (fig. 5). In keeping with VSBA's delight in contraries, the formality of the processional march is diluted by the two-dimensional Pop Art style arches above—school bus yellow on one side, Chinese cinnabar red on the reverse, all outlined with a serrated line recalling Medieval crenelated molding or Greek temple ornamentation. Notwithstanding the perversity of VSBA's architectural anomalies, anticipation and excitement do build as the visitor slowly ascends the monumental stair, transitioning from the tumult of the city outside—visible just beyond the adjacent bank of windows—to the art collection above.

Fig. 4 First Avenue lobby.

Some have called these the stairs that go nowhere.[17] For, once at the top, the space—which contains admission desk, store, handicap ramp, and steps to the second floor gallery—seemingly contains no means of ascending to the upper floors. Ignoring suggestions from its Seattle associates to continue the scale of the grand stair, VSBA instead designed a plain, utilitarian stairwell as the primary circulation route. Its unpretentious honesty and innocuous placement are a nice foil to the grand stair in theory, but problematic for the visitor in actuality. Elevators, discretely tucked some distance away in the interior spine of the galleries—initially without any sign at VSBA's behest—are neither intended nor capable of functioning as the primary means of reaching the third and fourth floor galleries. Thus, on a free day with five thousand visitors, circulation poses for everyone a problem.

According to Venturi, the rich resonance of architecture derives from its meaningful exercise of symbolism, complexity, and contradiction. Thus, the jumble of the entry foyer is succeeded by the solemn progression of the grand stairway to the second floor, the elegant Ming Dynasty sculptures are rendered askew by the slightly off-center Pop Art arches above them, and the maze of galleries on each of the upper floors is anchored by the spine of a gently curving central corridor. Ambiguity is produced at the First Avenue entrance by two sets of doors (one beckoning, the other repelling) and, once inside, by the fat column that momentarily blocks the visitor's progress.

Fig. 5 Grand stairway.

There is probably a reason VSBA has not produced the number of structures Venturi's success as an architectural writer would suggest: his philosophy is more intriguing than its realization. A building need not be pretty (SAM has been variously described as looking like a department store, a storage warehouse, and a fortress), nor consistent as opposed to disjunctive. It is even okay for a structure to eschew the comfortable or to celebrate non-functioning elements. Those devices that impede the actual functioning of this museum as a public building, on the other hand, constitute a real flaw.

Venturi's description of SAM as an "urban art museum" presupposes availability and popular ease of access—those very attributes VSBA has taken pains to circumscribe. Once inside, movement becomes frustratingly obstructed. In these days of MTV and instant gratification, the general public is easily discouraged by such architectural games. According to local architectural associate Jim Olson, few Seattlites like their museum building. The popularity SAM enjoys is attributable to its genial management and lively programming, and is abetted by the physical alterations to the building instigated by staff. As though heeding the "Desiderata," the museum has changed those things it could (closing down the Second Avenue entry and making the entrance foyer less confusing) and accepted those that it is powerless to correct (the weight-bearing column).[18]

SAM's design flaws are due to misguided—not sinister—intentions on the part of its eastern establishment architects, and perhaps to their arrogant presumption that they knew what was best for this "little hick town"[19] in the west. Even so, VSBA imbued the "seriously whimsical"[20] museum with many charming elements and these have been emphasized (fig. 6). Borofsky's ink black silhouette sets off the intricate patterning of the polychromatic façade. Children gather on the great stair beneath monumental reclining camels. Chamber music is performed in the cathedral-like space below chrome yellow arches. Tubes of neon light, randomly installed by a local artist around exterior window panes one Christmas, have been retained year-round because they resonate with contemporary ornamentation and speak to an audience the museum wishes to attract. An instance of SAM's management genius in going with the flow, this decorative addition is one Venturi, Scott Brown and Associates would love.

Fig. 6 A seriously whimsical museum.

1 Richard Meier refers to the work of Robert Venturi as "honky-tonk populism" in his book, *Building the Getty* (New York: Alfred A. Knopf, 1997), 28.

2 Janet Y. Abrams, "Contemplation and Congregation in the Popular Urban Art Museum: Two Projects by Venturi, Rauch & Scott Brown," *Lotus International* 55 (1987): 85.

3 I am speaking metonymically, since in choosing Venturi, they were choosing the firm VSBA.

4 Robert Venturi, *Complexity and Contradiction in Architecture*, 2nd ed. (New York: Museum of Modern Art, 1977).

5 Robert Venturi, Denise Scott Brown, and Steven Izenour, *Learning from Las Vegas*, rev. ed. (Cambridge: MIT Press, 1977).

6 "Seattle Art Museum: City Adding a Jewel," *Seattle Times*, 1 December 1991.

7 Robert Venturi, "Diversity, Relevance and Representation in Historicism, or Plus Ça Change ... Plus a Plea for Pattern All Over Architecture with a Postscript on My Mother's House," *Architectural Record* (June 1982): 115.

8 Pierluigi Nicolin, "The Context as Collage: The Decorative Response of Robert Venturi in Seattle," *Lotus International* 74 (1992): 86-97.

9 VSBA envisioned the museum's grand staircase as a piazza linking an extended city walk or passage way: pedestrians would be drawn from the business area above, down through the museum and the Harbor Steps to the wharf at water's edge.

10 Venturi, Scott Brown, and Izenour, *Learning from Las Vegas*, 87.

11 Fredric Jameson, *Postmodernism or, the Cultural Logic of Late Capitalism* (Durham: Duke University Press, 1997), 101.

12 Abrams, 95.

13 Gail Joice, Seattle Art Museum Senior Deputy Director, interview by author, tape recording, Seattle, WA, 13 March 1998.

14 Sylvia Lavin writes, "Entering a museum now involves a whole series of rituals, buying tickets, check ing coats, noticing the museum store; and various technical requirements often necessitate placing the galleries on upper floors, such that access to a museum no longer means fairly immediate access to works of art." She quotes Venturi as referring to this consequence as "the remoteness of art." Sylvia Lavin, "Venturi, Rauch and Scott Brown Disclose the Plans for Three New Museum Projects, Showing Complexity and Tradition in Design for the Viewing of Art," *Interiors* 147 (November 1987): 166.

15 Joice, interview.

16 *Ibid.*

17 Peter Staten, "Serious Whimsy," *Seattle Weekly*, 11 December 1991, 58.

18 The museum visually minimized the obstacle by changing its color from bright blue to white.

19 Jim Olson, Olson and Sundberg Architects, interview by author, tape recording, Seattle, WA, 13 March 1998.

20 Staten, 52.

Karen Lansky

San Francisco Museum of Modern Art: from Civic Center to civic center

We think of San Francisco as a premiere destination, one of the world's incomparable cities. So when the board of directors of the San Francisco Museum of Modern Art (SFMOMA) decided to leave the Civic Center and build a new museum at Yerba Buena Gardens, they aspired to nothing less: they wanted a premiere destination, an incomparable building—a world-class museum at the heart of a new arts community. They envisioned an enormous exhibition space for contemporary art, which tends to large installations. And they wanted the entire structure to have humanist appeal—warm, welcoming, but physically amenable to an array of commercial ventures, from social events in the lobby and lectures and shows in the theater, to the ever more obligatory bookstore and cafe. The metaphor, later stunningly realized, was "magnet by day, beacon by night."

The building that grew from these early plans could hardly have been conceived in a less auspicious setting. Yet it is that setting alone that accounts for the transformation SFMOMA has stamped on its environs. The city of San Francisco once operated a venereal disease clinic in the space where SFMOMA now stands. The clinic occupied a dismal storefront within the monotonous Victorian grid of flophouses, pawnshops, and liquor stores called Skid Row. City Hall, however, had long noted the strategic downtown location of the eyesore and had sweeping plans to bring in culture and commerce. Once SFMOMA decided to become part of the growing cultural movement downtown, it abandoned the futile elitism of its old Civic Center home and changed direction in more ways than one. The museum's choice of a dramatic new building, huge and powerful in form, announced SFMOMA as the main player in the free-wheeling mix of architecture at Yerba Buena Gardens. With cafe tables and chairs spilling onto the sidewalk, the museum's presence further changed the function of the surrounding neighborhood—it drew people in and infused the community with vigor and significance. In the wake of its own metamorphosis, SFMOMA led the transformation of the useless and despised streets south of Market into a cultural resource available to everyone—a real civic center.

Fig. 1 San Francisco Museum of Modern Art.

Fig. 2 Museum lobby.

As such, the building pays a double dividend: its multifaceted interior serves as an enclosed civic center as well. The modest entry opens onto a soaring lobby designed to double as a social hall—or a piazza (fig. 2). Cafe, bookstore, theater, elevators, coatcheck, telephones, education rooms, and an all-purpose room are deployed around the perimeter such that the eye takes them in at a glance. The all-purpose room is used as everything from a dining hall to a boardroom because the museum directors did not want to waste money on a special place to hold a meeting. The bonus: from the all-purpose room they can observe visitors using the services offered throughout the lobby. The lobby-cum-civic-center is both self-contained and open to the world outside. Looking across it to the bookstore or cafe, visitors receive a full report of doings streetside, including the weather, thanks to enormous plate glass windows.

The person responsible for the museum's unusual interplay of exterior and interior, of form and function, is Mario Botta, a Lugano-born architect who had never built in the U.S. before winning the SFMOMA commission. The museum chose Botta because his philosophy of architecture accorded with their goals, and his attention to spatial dominance expressed their ambitions. When designing a museum, a country house, or a cathedral, Botta's aim is to dominate the chosen site and lay claim to its territory with a unique and powerful stamp intended to define future development in the area. His plan for SFMOMA was big and bold, in a style absolutely new to the city's architectural lexicon. There is no trace of the surrounding styles San Franciscans have come to accept—the Spanish Colonial, the ubiquitous bay-windowed Victorian, the Art Deco of the Pacific Bell towers that rise behind the new museum, or the Post-Modern "Jukebox" Marriott across the street. Instead, SFMOMA takes its cue from the Italian-Swiss sensibilities of Botta, whose fortress-like structures echo the Romanesque and vernacular tradition of his native Ticino.

Botta blends the spare symmetry of European rationalism with the earthiness of his native soil. He builds with stones, bricks, and mortar to create the feeling of ancient walls, all the while adhering to the rigorous geometry of his mentors, Louis Kahn and Le Corbusier. His buildings are wedded to the vocabulary of Modernism, each an homage to the square, the circle, the triangle. In SFMOMA those geometric forms are aggressively expressed as a stepped-back triad of solid rectangles wedged apart by a cylinder into two horizontal blocks of symmetrical perfection. Because he prefers to build solid stone walls, Botta has been accused of creating an architecture that turns its back on the world and shuts it out. He himself claims to use architecture not simply to escape the ugliness of the present-day city, but as a "way of resisting a loss of identity, a way of resisting banalization. It's always a question of making any new intervention an integral part of the cultural and historical situation of the site."[1]

In San Francisco, a deceptively simple sheath of crenelated, rustic sienna brick is both the secret of the building's strength and the basis for its integration into the site. Patterned in vertical designs, spaced in string courses that appear as horizontal black lines, contrasted against bands of elegant black and white striping, brick supplies the elegant, elemental warmth that controls and overcomes surrounding architectural clutter (fig. 1). The museum's streetscale entry respects the area's commercial environment and relieves visitors from having to make sudden, perhaps unwelcome, emotional accommodation to a grand entrance. The same cohesive program of color and design extends internally to knit together the functions of the museum's various operations.

Botta's preoccupation with light in his conception of SFMOMA seems to have evolved from his ideas for the

Evry Cathedral in France, which he finished in 1988, a year before beginning the museum. Evry consists only of a sheared-off cylindrical shape, open at the top to admit sunlight and the slow passage of the seasons. The oculus at Evry is surrounded by trees, a favorite motif Botta wanted to use again around the oculus at the museum, much against the wishes of the client board of directors, who insisted on simplicity and clean design. Pierluigi Nicolin, in an interview with Botta, cites the similarity between Evry and SFMOMA, explaining that Botta uses his circles in "many guises."[2]

Fig. 3 Turret bridge below the oculus with floodlights mounted on arch for night lighting.

At the museum, Botta placed the sheared cylinder of Evry inside a cube to create another familiar theme, the hollowed-out block that creates space by utilizing the relationship between inside and outside. The client wanted Botta to challenge the tradition of museum-as-palace and reinvent SFMOMA in an entirely new form: the museum-as-community-center. This meant a fusing of art and commerce, always odious to purists. From another point of view, it meant enhancing the function and public experience of the museum by adding educational facilities and expanding revenue producers like the cafe and bookstore. Further, it meant conceptualizing all commercial space as multi-purpose and open to community use. SFMOMA needed this radical mission change to turn a formerly aloof and inaccessible museum into a magnet capable of pulling isolated skid row into the heart of the city. To that end, Botta's adaptation of the theme at Evry seems particularly suited to his goals of congregation and shared experience.

Botta observes that social disintegration—principally the loss of shared experience—has intensified the spiritual role of the museum, shifting it to that of the cathedral of yesterday. He sees the modern museum as "a space dedicated to witnessing and searching for a new religiosity... a place of common encounter and confrontation."[3] As daylight streams through the huge oculus at the top of the atrium, bathes the upper floors, and glows into the lobby, SFMOMA looks and feels like a cathedral. The insularity of that cathedral-like space, however, has been artfully designed also to merge seamlessly with the museum's social and economic needs. For instance, Botta refers to the first floor lobby as a *piazza el fresco*, a device he used at the Evry Cathedral for the gathering of the congregation. At the cathedral, light enters from only one source, the round aperture above, creating a sense of direct heavenly communication. At SFMOMA, strong searchlights mounted on a bridge transform the museum itself into an agent of illumination as they send beams of light through the oculus and back into the city night. Botta has thereby imbued the museum with layers of metaphorical significance while building into it the physical presence and power of a beacon.

The visitor leaves the worldly realm of the piazza by means of the black granite central staircase that rises behind the information counters. The staircase is introduced by three massive columns, clad at the base in alter-

Fig. 4 Visitors at outdoor tables of the museum's cafe lighting.

nate zones of polished and matte black stone. Botta refers to the grand staircase as the "stairs to the apartments," underlining his concept of the lobby and galleries as comprising a small village within walls.

Some criticize the staircase as insufficiently monumental; nevertheless, it serves discreetly to convey visitors four floors up the ever-whiter, simpler, sunlit atrium space into proximity with the dazzling oculus. The higher one climbs, the more challenging the artwork becomes—more contemporary, larger. At the top, installations can take up an entire room. Indeed, one portion of an installation was mistaken for actual unfinished lathe and plaster work. To regulate the amount of light, Botta designed photo-sensitive glass window blinds for the ceiling that move with the sun. It is interesting to note, standing at the top of the central atrium known as the turret, that this highest, brightest, whitest part of the building is home to the most abstract and cerebral art on display, as if its association with thought more than matter was appropriate to the highest regions of the museum. A translucent bridge bisects the turret below the oculus, arousing uneasy curiosity about one's nearness to the unknown (fig. 3). Botta's top floor design for contemporary exhibitions gives the space a pared-down, unearthly feel while subliminally announcing it as the most important one in the museum, a rarified domain proper to SFMOMA's main interest, contemporary art.

The top floor windows open to views of Twin Peaks and the surrounding cultural complex. On the floor below, incised like an embrasure into the atrium wall, a tiny opening reveals a sliver of the world outside. Richard Young, Project Manager from Bechtel Engineering, says the size of that window raised a point of contention: the client wanted a bigger one to make a more emphatic visual statement. Botta remained unusually adamant on this point, insisting that he needed the oblong opening, or *apertio*, to define the volume of the wall. As part of the language of a Botta building, the *apertio* is mysteriously proper to a medieval fortress. It raises disturbing issues about what is being defended, and from whom, while giving the viewer precious little access to an answer.

Back at the piazza, however, giant plate glass windows open onto the panorama of the street in both the bookstore and cafe areas. "I tried to escape the anonymity of the glass curtain wall and the International Style," claims Botta, whose own idea of Modernism avoids quotation as much as possible.[4] Instead, Botta's fortress-like exterior creates a medieval sense of enclosure. Visitors spiral down gradually from the vertiginous and sacred cathedral space above to the peopled environs of the public space below. Each level of descent brings closer the sound of voices and the aroma of food in the lobby, until the last turn on the grand staircase gently reintroduces the everyday world of SFMOMA's commercial ventures.

From the sidewalk, the plate glass "walls" of the bookstore and Cafe Museo look like department store display windows. But at SFMOMA the view goes both ways. Botta's attention to people as objects on display stresses the provisional quality of the border and its perplexing power to construct meaning in the liminal space, often making ambiguous exactly what is inside and what is outside. In his essay, "The Exhibitionary Complex," Tony Bennett expands upon Foucault's view of places of confinement as

Fig. 5 Front view of museum as seen from the Yerba Buena Center for the Visual Arts.

institutional articulations of power and knowledge relations. He writes, "Museums may have enclosed objects within walls, but the nineteenth century saw their doors opened to the general public—witnesses who are essential to the display of power."[5] At SFMOMA, such display includes Botta's carefully choreographed setting for seeing and being seen. Inside, cafe patrons enjoy the spectacle of passing streetlife and the little dramas unfolding at outdoor tables (fig. 4), while the "witnesses" who comprise that streetlife are confronted with the power of the display as it is presented on either side of the plate glass border. Simply entering the museum's cafe, or taking a seat at an outside table, confers cultural status. The power of this "inside" role is illustrated in the care taken by the "general public" to look at, but not touch, patrons on display.

Botta's territorial intentions—to claim and define the site—can be seen in the physical impact of the building upon the surrounding community. Because it encloses over 225,000 square feet, second in scale only to the Museum of Modern Art, SFMOMA seems oversized. Young says Botta would have made the museum even larger if he had been given the space. To resolve the problem of proportion, Botta used the vertical thrust of the soaring Pacific Bell towers behind the museum to counter its aggressive bulk, and their delicate granite tracery to complement the symmetrical, stepped-back rectangular grouping of the brick façade. To imagine the museum without the towers is to sense the monolithic brutalism city planners of the 1960s sought so long to avoid. By fitting the two buildings together visually, the "new intervention," in Botta's words, becomes "an integral part of the cultural and historical situation of the site."[6]

Since its planning stages in the early 1960s, development of Yerba Buena Gardens was always meant to be carefully coordinated. But because it was the domain of several entities and never a monolithic project, some parts were completed before others had even been approved, and much remains to be built. The vagaries of city planning have foiled some of Botta's best laid plans. The architect intended SFMOMA's signature oculus to be a brightly-lit eye guarding the downtown. The eye looks instead onto the back of the Yerba Buena Arts complex across the street, a block-long concrete wall relieved only by a small path leading into the gardens. Thus no direct rapport exists between the two buildings.

For Botta, confusion and contradiction of this sort are the architectural bane of the modern city. He discusses such disintegration of the urban landscape with Pierluigi Nicolin in *Mario Botta: Architecture 1980-1990.* Nicolin regards the post-war city as an unplanned, unintegrated urban disaster. Botta replies that urban planning will always be determined more by political choices having to do with economics, and that these have nothing to do with the destiny of any specific piece of land. He feels responsible for the urban fabric and says, "I, too, have observed this tendency of architects to flee from whatever responsibilities do not fall strictly within their own territorial boundaries."[7] Similarly, in a letter to Mrs. Watari apropos of his design for the Watari-Um museum in Tokyo, Botta refers to his project as a "confrontation" with the city: "From the first drawing I followed a strong and precise course that had to resist the confusion and contradiction of languages, styles and forms present in Tokyo."[8] Elsewhere Botta speaks of "lacerations inflicted by new urban interventions," and indeed is appalled by the unplanned urban mélange that so invigorates Robert Venturi.[9]

Yet the "confusion and contradiction" of architecture in San Francisco, such as the disjunctions of SFMOMA with Fumihiko Maki's Yerba Buena Arts Center, and both with the gaudy splendor of the Post-Modern "Jukebox Marriott," seem to inspire their own solutions. For instance, Botta contrived the front entrance of SFMOMA (fig. 5) to face the path that leads into the Visual Arts Center across the street, connecting the two with a simple crosswalk. Visitors have discovered that if they walk fifty feet or so up the path into the arts complex, and then turn to look back at the museum, they are rewarded with a view of its symmetry aligned perfectly against the surrounding buildings. A boat-shaped piece of sculpture quoting the nearby waterfront stands right at the spot where they must stop, so the sculpture is suddenly seen as well. And then, since they are on the path, people move along it into the garden to discover greenery softening the spiked arcs of the Marriott's roofline. Thus the putative border is breached again, this time by the illusion of landscape interpenetrating architecture.

In San Francisco, serendipity has a way of correcting the best laid plans. Today, just as Mario Botta intended, SFMOMA dominates the fluid, sophisticated urban mix at Yerba Buena Center. But tomorrow the Jewish and Mexican museums will go up. Plans are to paint the Mexican Museum tomato red. Who can predict the effect of red paint on Botta's powerful sienna brick façade? A photography museum and more galleries will glorify the remaining dismal nineteenth-century storefronts on Mission Street. As a group they are likely to infuse Yerba Buena Center with an organic dynamism greater than the power of any one building.

Mario Botta produced a premiere destination. By succeeding as a magnet for people and new commercial ventures, SFMOMA gives the area civic purpose. "South of Market" no longer means blight; it stands for SoMa, the city's newest cultural enterprise.

1 Pierluigi Nicolin, *Mario Botta: Buildings and Projects 1961-1982* (New York: Rizzoli International Publications, 1984), 36.
2 Zahid Sardar, "Rounding Off The Block," *San Francisco Examiner Magazine,* 15 January 1995, 12.
3 Stuart Wrede, *Mario Botta* (New York: Museum of Modern Art, 1986), 65.
4 Sardar, 13.
5 Tony Bennett, "The Exhibitionary Complex," in *Thinking About Exhibitions* ed. Reesa Greenberg, Bruce W. Ferguson, and Sandy Nairne (London, New York: Routledge, 1996), 82.
6 Wrede, 65.
7 Quoted by Werner Oechslin and Pierluigi Nicolin, in *Mario Botta: Architecture 1980-1990* (Barcelona: Editorial Gustavo Ceili, S.A., 1991), 23.
8 Quoted in an essay on Botta's design for the Watari-Um museum, by James Steele, in *Museum Builders* (London: Academy Group, Ltd., 1994), 39.
9 Etsuko Watari, *Mario Botta: Watari-Um Project in Tokyo 1985-90* (Tokyo: Watari-Um Museum, 1990), 8.

Karen Lansky

The Skirball Cultural Center: The Paradox of Intent

In Los Angeles, the 405 Freeway crosses under Muholland Drive at the summit of Sepulveda Pass in the Santa Monica Mountains. A generation ago, the Mulholland exit emptied into the woodsy confines of upper Brentwood and Bel Air, northern outposts of westside wealth strung along Mulholland's south ridge. On the north slope of that fabled ridge lay the equally woodsy Encino and Sherman Oaks, San Fernando Valley counterparts of their westside neighbors. Since the 1960s the area has become a kind of four corners of West Los Angeles affluence, an unofficial preferred location for private schools, religious and cultural institutions. The pass was also uncrowded—until recently. Slowly, its rustic charm has been transformed by perfectly worthy institutions vying for a piece of paradise. One of the latest is the Skirball Cultural Center.

The Skirball Cultural Center is made up of seven or nine distinct building areas, depending on how many rooflines you are counting, with an additional building, the multipurpose Great Hall, to be completed in 2000. These areas house the Discovery Center, a nationally-recognized hands-on learning exhibition for children, the museum galleries, the bookstore and lobby, the restaurant, a round auditorium, and the administrative and educational wing. The Skirball sits on a shallowly graded shoulder that abuts on the ridge of the Santa Monica Mountains where the Sepulveda Boulevard tunnel runs under Mulholland Drive. Locals never thought the land was buildable before the Skirball started to go up. It was too small, just a curve in the road, a collecting point for cast-off sofas and tires. The wonder of it was why anyone would choose to erect a building there, let alone a "village" of imposing architecture shoe-horned into the side of the mountain.

Fig. 1 Exterior of Skirball Cutural Center, facing west across Sepulveda Boulevard.

The Skirball Cultural Center is the realized dream of its founding president and CEO, Dr. Uri Herscher. Located adjacent to the University of Southern California campus until 1995, the Skirball Museum was given over mainly to displays chronicling the history of the Jewish people, hands-on activities for children, and a gift store. Herscher himself took the lead in raising the money to build a new facility so that the rich museum collection could be used to better present every artistic and social aspect of Jewish life. As to location, he says he wanted to find a little left-over piece of land situated equidistant as possible between the city and the valley, which would, in fact, place the Center at the center of Jewish life in Los Angeles. "When I saw this place," says Herscher, gesturing towards the mountains, "I thought how much like Israel it was—a small, neglected place that could be made to grow and bloom. I called it 'Promised Land West,' exactly mid-way between the valley and the city, in a no-man's land."[1] These ideas are knit together by a notion long held in Jewish consciousness, almost diasporic in its origins, that the unlanded and dispersed must work to piece together what remnants they own, what beliefs they share, to form a whole that promises continuity. Centuries of rootlessness have transformed their ability, equally as a point of pride and as the ultimate challenge, to make "something out of nothing" into a kind of ethos. The new Skirball Cultural Center has great symbolic significance for Herscher, not only physically, but spiritually as well: it signifies the root of the immigrant experience for him. "The main purpose of the Skirball Cultural Center is to tell the story of the Jewish people from antiquity to the present day, with particular emphasis on the American experience," he says. "The core exhibition is not about objects. It uses objects to tell a story. My story was discontinued, but I can find pieces of my identity here. This place gives it back to me; it fills in the gaps."[2]

Fig. 2 Front entry.

Fig. 3 Detail of inner courtyard.

Architecturally, that story begins with the Sukkah-like structure that is at the main entrance to the Center (fig. 2). The trellis at the entry symbolizes the Sukkah, a three-sided arbor that Jews construct in the open air during harvest season to celebrate the holiday of Succoth, during which they give thanks for God's bounty. The Sukkah, decorated with all manner of fruits and vegetables and plants, becomes an outdoor dining area during the week of Succoth (Tabernacles). For Herscher, the Sukkah is more than a metaphor. It represents in a traditional way the ingathering of people, a place for sharing and togetherness. The trellis emphasizes the spirit of welcome at the entrance to the Skirball. The architecture, however, takes its quotations from a larger cultural landscape. Ultimately, it expresses the complex experience of immigration to America.

Herscher and the man he chose as architect, Moshe Safdie, are both immigrants to North America. They left Israel as young boys and share a long friendship. They share a romance with the garden, especially with the long-held Middle Eastern belief that everyone should have a garden. They also believe in the oasis that blooms in the desert as an analogue to the blossoming of the modern State of Israel. When they decided to work together on the Skirball Cultural Center, Herscher and Safdie agreed to incorporate this image into the program. They chose a plain material, concrete, as a complement to nature, and stainless steel panels to reflect the sky. Safdie describes his architectural intentions thus:

> *I needed to create containment, a sense of place, which I accomplished with the courtyards. My breakthrough was in recognizing that the building was not alone; the hills were there. I needed to bring in the hills. So, the courtyards only have three sides; the fourth side is the hill. One side is always nature. An unexpected benefit was that the building acted as a sound barrier as it opened to quiet nature. My intention was to work with the site, not against it. Because it was so fragile, I took a more Greek than a Roman approach.*[3]

Fig. 4 Streetside wall.

At the Skirball, expression of this garden ethos in the characteristics of the building itself could be described as not unlike the Sabra, a native fruit—but also the name for a native Israeli—tough on the outside, soft on the inside (fig. 3).

The Skirball offers this paradox of intent: its mission is to be warm, open, and welcoming, but its exterior appearance suggests a cool impenetrability. It is a haven of peace and fellowship hunkered down against the hillside like a cement and stainless steel bunker. It is open to all, but its identity and function are initially unreadable. The concrete amphitheater is presumably a prop against mudslides, and the rear wall a barrier against incursions from the mountain itself. Yet, as of now, they and the ensemble of other structures settle into the soft green hills with all the grace of a retaining wall, and seem on guard even against those hills (fig. 4).

Safdie admits that the location of the Skirball makes it a place that no one will ever approach on foot. Nevertheless, he designed a traditional entrance with a central staircase that steps down to a motor court. A sidewalk fronts the motor court, but no direct access from the motorcourt to the sidewalk exists. Instead, a low wall curves around the street side of the motor court, forming a barrier between the street and the traditional entrance. On second glance, a pass-through as big as an afterthought pierces the curved wall, but a strong sense of you-can't-get-there-from-here frustration lingers, especially as one hurries by in a car. This misapprehension of the first-time visitor is a sensitive issue, given the ideal of welcome-to-all motivating the architectural design. Herscher claims that inaccessibility of any sort was never Safdie's original intention.

Fig. 5 Lobby, facing inner courtyard.

Originally, Safdie planned a traditional front entrance to receive visitors walking to the Skirball from a proposed parking lot across Sepulveda Boulevard via a crosswalk with a light. The entrance provided a sense of place where no other such reference existed. During construction, Safdie's plan temporarily fell victim to the whims of the City of Los Angeles, which revoked permission for the crosswalk, leaving the front entrance virtually irrelevant. Visitors are accordingly forced to use the parking lot next to the building, then to hunt around for a way to the courtyard and front entrance. Unfortunately, that way was via an unmarked sidedoor, which Herscher describes as a "typical Middle Eastern entrance, almost invisible, unassuming." If visitors missed the sidedoor, they had to walk around the parking lot, out to the street and down to the front of the building to get inside. A first-time visitor exiting the freeway was hard-pressed to know where to go. Herscher and Safdie wrestled with this inexplicable predicament for two years before the city reversed its ruling and reinstated the crosswalk. The parking lot, dotted with dozens of mature sycamores, went in a week later (fig. 5).

In fall of 1998, construction began on the newest phase of the complex, the Great Hall surmounting three subterranean parking levels on the north side of the complex where the original parking lot used to be. A new underground parking structure will link the Great Hall to the Skirball's main entrance by a pathway curving down around the main building and ending at the motor court. Herscher and Safdie say they will then modify the main entrance for easy access from the parking lot across the street as well. As it now stands, the building's axiality is unclear. The question is whether the Great Hall will give the complex the order and balance it needs, or cause it to intrude even more into the environment.

Fig. 6 Detail of stainless steel panel.

The paradox of intent perseveres. If Safdie is emotionally tied to the organic and verdant, why has he made the building massive and impenetrable (fig. 6)? Both Herscher and Safdie would say, look again. The heavy trellises are there to support the growth of plants and thus soften the overall appearance. And, in fact, the retaining walls are already covered with the ameliorating green of ficus. The hard surfaces of the building function, then partly as a scaffold for the overflowing garden. Inside the Skirball, one finds this softness in situ: balconies brimming with plants and a pond with water lilies. Every window frames the hills. The freeway on the other side of the thick walls is banished from sight and sound—and from thought.

Herscher argues for the unobtrusive, even somewhat hidden, entrances to Middle Eastern architecture, for the unpretentious doorway leading to a hospitable interior, as an important confirmation of the human need—of Jew and non-Jew alike—to belong, to be welcomed as part of a group. But there is a big difference between intention and what people see when they drive by. One wonders if the Skirball can resolve the paradox and fit the building to the left-over piece of land it occupies so that it beckons outsiders to come in. The Skirball Cultural Center, however, is a work-in-progress, evolving architecturally and environmentally almost on a daily basis. As its landscaping grows it will surely take on a different character. In the garden environment that Herscher and Safdie envisioned, nature, after all, will have the last word in the architectural program.

1 Dr. Uri Herscher, interview by author, in person, Los Angeles, CA, 12 October 1998.
2 *Ibid.*
3 Moshe Safdie, interview by author, by phone, Los Angeles, CA, 18 October 1998.

Charles A. Lagreco

The Getty Center and the Limits of Architecture: Access Interruptus?

The Getty Museum has been the subject of innumerable articles describing in detail the complications and constraints that faced the project team, marveling on the enormity of the budget, and expressing superlatives in admiration of the final product. Kenneth Frampton has spoken of the importance for the historian in gaining a critical perspective that can only come with time. This does not prevent a discussion of the validity of the Getty program and design solution, but it tempers judgment and calls for restraint in final conclusions. What seems clear is that this complex and ambitious project raises substantial questions about the responsibilities and role of the museum in our culture and what constitutes an appropriate architectural response.

Richard Meier, for those of us who were educated as architects in the 1960s, represented an orthodoxy that carried on from the Corbusian legacy through the English to American Architectural Schools, and inevitably on to new generations of architectural students—a legacy which has exposed and informed, while uplifting the expression of functional abstraction to high art. It was with some apprehension that I learned of Meier's selection as the principal architect for the Getty Center, both because of what I knew of the aspirations of the Institution, and of the site selected and its implications for Los Angeles. Living virtually in the shadow of the site, I could watch as the Brentwood foothills were reconfigured, recompacted, and stabilized, as my friend and colleague Emmet Wemple peppered the hillside with new trees on elaborate terraced slopes, and aggressively shaped the hills in the undeveloped area between the adjoining residential neighborhood and the always active San Diego Freeway. Finally I could observe the growth of individual buildings, sprouting with a deliberate, if not always clarified order, at a scale that dwarfed its surroundings. The complex sits presently with authority and an air of permanence, on a site visible from many parts of the city, the buildings' uneasy imposition on the hills gradually softening with the assertion of the evolving landscape (fig.1).

Fig. 1 View of the Getty from the south in a residential neighborhood

Kevin Starr talks about California Architecture as an architecture of "wannabe's,"[1] an apt description for those drawn to the state by the power of the Hollywood myth, and characteristic of the eclectic range of architectural styles that represent the regional heritage of this island on the land, of the hothouse of exotica that allows almost anything to take root with the proper nutrients and care. The Getty, with a confidence that comes from massive endowments, spread huge dollops of funding on the project from its inception. Who better to provide an international home for the Getty, than Meier, the easterner, who with his impeccable international credentials could complete the final transformation of a private idiosyncratic art collection into the mammoth global juggernaut that the Getty Trust had become. Discussion about the Getty Center's relationship to the community must inevitably focus on the choice of site and architect, and what it tells us about the institution and its motives. Since the commitment to the site had been made long before Meier came aboard as architect, its development was not an option for discussion but the Faustian bargain that came with the commission.

Harold Williams, who served as President and CEO of the Getty Trust during the projects implementation, summarized the Getty Center's intentions as wanting "to be timeless and a work of art in itself, because to the outside world the Getty Center makes a statement about what the Getty is at its core.... The structures set an example of enduring artistic quality."[2] The architecture of museums has undergone significant reexamination in the last twenty years and Meier has been part of that process. If the Renzo Piano and Richard Rogers's Centre Pompidou reduced the museum to the cultural equivalent of the marketplace, and the building type to that of the department store, then, thankfully, there were alternative voices such as Hollein's Municipal Museum at Monchengladbach, which envisions the museum complex as a landscape of buildings, each with its individual character incorporated in an urban design scheme that is totally connected to the city and the landscape. According to Heinrich Klotz, Meier's role in this dialogue was "to continue in the abstract traditions of Modernism, to preserve the purity of the movement's gleaming newness even at the very end of the 20th Century."[3] While these comments relate to the Frankfurt museum project, it is instructive to see Meier's position against the context of the Getty's quest for architectural excellence as a reflection of the quality of its collection. What was clearly not desired, however, was for the architecture to influence the objects to be displayed. Stephen Rountree, in *Making Architecture, The Getty Center*, describes the exhibition spaces as being modeled after the Dulwich Gallery and with proportions suited to older works of art. Rountree puts a positive spin on this "clash of disparate points of view"[4] as a collaborative effort, but New York architect, Thurry Despont, was brought in initially to design the period galleries, and later as facilitator and intermediary between Meier and the Museum. In many respects, while technically brilliant, the galleries are the least integrated portions of Meier's composition, having neither the formal consistency nor the familiar circulation driven matrix that usually characterizes Meier's mature work. Meier speaks of the random circulation as an attempt to allow for exploration and discovery, but the results are more nearly confusion and disorientation.

Richard Meier's statement of intentions, assigns primary responsibility for the form of the Getty Center to its hilltop site, "accessible to the flow of urban life and yet slightly removed from the city."[5] For those who have somehow remained unexposed to the unprecedented level of publicity and attention given the Center in its formative stages, the site is a portion of previously inaccessible land in the foothills of the Santa Monica Mountains bordering the Sepulveda Pass. The Pass, along with its sister, the Cahuenga Pass, provides the opportunity to connect the two major developed areas of the Los Angeles metropolitan area: the San Fernando Valley with the greater Los Angeles Basin. The site, located at the mouth of the Sepulveda Pass, has a commanding view that swings from downtown west to the ocean and from Palos Verdes north to Malibu. The artery for this connection is the San Diego Freeway, which occupies the low ground in the pass and generates a constant, relentless flow of traffic adjacent to the site; eight to ten lanes of freeway supported by a parallel road. Perpendicular to the freeway along the base of the foothills runs Sunset Boulevard, which winds from downtown to the Pacific. Paralleling it, on the uppermost ridge of the mountains, meanders the continuation of Mulholland Drive. Between these two roads the canyons and ridges are too steep for any more than exploratory intrusions, and the tops of the mountains are inaccessible except for the most determined hiker. Private residential sanctuaries vie for choice view lots on private cul-de-sac streets, which branch off the canyon and ridge access roads that are disconnected from the urban grid in the valley below. A similar clash of public and institutional uses in a residential area occurred with the original Getty Museum when it was built in the 1970s next to the Getty Mansion in Malibu. An overlay of restrictions on public access and activities was negotiated to allow the Museum to coexist in a residential context. The Getty chose to follow this model of residential exclusivity when it purchased the Brentwood property in the early 1980s seemingly only faintly aware of the magnitude of what was to follow.

Fig. 2. The two axes of the San Diego freeway.

Fig. 3. Pierre Koenig's Case Study House #22 (1960).

Meier describes the site as having two axes along the ridge, one relating to the freeway and one to the street grid below, providing a formal connection to the city. It would be more accurate to say that the Center reflects the geometry of the freeway at the point where it turns and plunges into the developed urban grid below in the basin, that grid in turn reinforcing the ridgelines of the site (fig. 2). Whether referring to the freeway shift or the city street pattern, these two grids are more about the methodology Meier has developed to introduce complexity within a reductive vocabulary, than as a response to the formal nature of the city beyond. The site breaks free of the city and provides an overview; in Meier's words, "it overlooks the geometry of Los Angeles, which is spread like a vast, elegant carpet below the rugged terrain."[6] It is precisely this detachment that was integral in the initial strategy to locate on this site, and forms the inherent contradiction characterizing the Getty Center's relationship to the community. Meier captures the paradox by describing "the hilltop site of the Getty Center [as] offer[ing] the best place to see and understand Los Angeles."[7] The city in Meier's terms is an abstraction best seen from above like the view from airplanes approaching LAX on a clear night, the infinite extension of lights overlaid by streams of white and red lights flowing down the arteries of traffic in endless vistas. This is the iconic view of Los Angeles firmly established in our lexicon by Julius Shulman's photograph of Pierre Koenig's Case Study House #22 (fig.3). It is an image of utopian clarity, idealized and secure, floating serenely above the city, the urban grid delineated and following the principles of perspective but giving no suggestion of the reality of the life below. A powerful image, yet hardly the mechanism to understand the true nature of the city below. Even if the view from the Getty hill is intended to reference the formal organization of the city, it lacks, however magnificent, the connectivity to clarify these characteristics. Meier describes his site strategy, thus:

> *In my view, there are two ways in which a building may be related to its site: one is to make it textually similar, to imitate what is already there; the other is to allow the buildings to acknowledge the more general aspects of the context, to order it in such a way that it recognizes and responds to its surroundings, and invites a reciprocal involvement.*[8]

The museum of necessity presents itself in two images to the public: in approach, as a mountain top monument seen obliquely and at significant distance, and at arrival, as an abstraction realized as a series of dramatic and sometimes confusing experiences, which confront the visitor in a direct tactile manner. While prominent and instantly recognizable, the Museum lacks both significance of place and coherence of form necessary to satisfy its status as monument. One has only to compare the Getty with the Griffith Park Observatory, whose massing and orientation to the street grid below anchors it to the city. The Museum complex and its supporting institutions are clearly detached from the city below and yet the visitor's experience is dominated by the anticipation of that site as an overlook to the city. Meier's buildings constantly frame and exploit these views. Existing at a distance, the city becomes an abstraction, which reduces the nature of the response to the Getty complex as a series of identifiable monuments with the city as background. This is a product of the highly ambiguous attitude that the Getty has toward its neighbors and to the community at large. When the Museum opened, banners suddenly appeared on Wilshire Boulevard, announcing the arrival of "Your Getty Museum." This orchestrated a public relations campaign, which succeeded beyond the Center's wildest nightmares. The unanticipated surge in attendance has created a logistics problem of enormous magnitude. Leisurely contemplative strolls through the Museum have been transformed into long lines for temporary exhibits, the café, the bookstore, the bathrooms. Even the central garden generates lines of visitors filing down the central circulation path. It is an attitude characterized by treating community relations as a public relation problem and by buying off whole neighborhoods through privatization of the already exclusive residential enclaves around the Museum site. Housing directly below the Getty has been gated and manned with security guards to prevent any public intrusion of naive tourists attempting to scale the grounds of the museum from below. It is virtually impossible to walk to the museum from the city because of the physical siting and the administrative obstacles placed in the way. After the Center opened, adjacent single family residents petitioned the city for posted restrictions to street parking. The approach by car is further restricted by a system of parking reservations that usually requires planning months ahead. Private shuttle services and a much-maligned public bus system provide some drop-in activity but the Getty makes it clear that this option is limited and clearly subservient to the reservation process. Robert Campbell, the Boston Globe architectural critic, has articulated what must be the most obvious yet damning of comments when he refers to the Getty Center as "hopelessly car dependent, another gated community.... Worse yet on this site the Getty can never legally expand. A setting in the city would have allowed for inevitable growth and change. The Getty's huge financial investment, by attracting further development around it, might have spun off some benefits for someone beside itself. The choice of site is an expression of institutional ego and self-importance."[9]

The selection of this site adjacent to an aggressive and politically empowered residential community with justifiable concerns about its new neighbor necessitated an involved process of negotiation on issues such as building mass, building height, lighting, noise, privacy, lines of site, traffic drainage and landscape issues. Even the choice of color had to be negotiated with the homeowner's associations. While the final public position puts a positive spin on these "collaborations," it seems clear that much of the architectural criticisms of the project relate back to the initial site decisions and the consequences of that strategy. Meier's European based Modernist vocabulary can be seen as having a direct link to the white international style of Richard Neutra and Rudolf Schindler in Southern California, a vocabulary that found its most eloquent expression in large private homes. Meier describes the elements of the Center with a clarity that belies the tremendous problems in accommodating the program to the site with its imposed constraints:

> *I had thought of stone as a way of grounding the buildings and giving them a sense of permanence. Stone has been used for retaining walls and the bases of all the buildings, and repetitive metal—a lighter, more fluid, less expensive material for cladding—have been utilized for the upper stories and curvilinear elements.*[10]

This strategy, entirely consistent with his Modernist heritage, is followed with considerable latitude as formal and programmatic pressures necessitated adjustments. To place the massive program on site within the height limitations, it was necessary to put over half the museum program below the stone base of the museum, which reinforces the defensive appearance of the Center's most public façades along the freeway and in neighborhoods to the south. Further, it was decided to use stone to completely enclose the Museum galleries rather than just provide a base, and this adds to the massive nature of these elements, relief coming from articulated fire stairs and protruding circulation elements. Most discordant is the use of stone for curtain wall elements, exposed frames, cantilevered wall planes, and freestanding columns, faced in the most textured travertine every quarried (fig.4). While the installation is a perfectly detailed technical tour-de-force, the underlying vocabulary is neither true to Meier's stated strategy nor to his roots. One wonders how his mentor, Marcel Breuer, would have responded to this syntactical problem. The Institute buildings are in comparison both more formally exciting and more responsive to the context and the architectural heritage of the region. They demonstrate the genius of a master architect at the height of his creative ability, working comfortably within the constraints of the program and site without artistic compromise. The disjointed qualities of the Center were reinforced by the unfortunate transference of responsibility for the central garden from Meier's deft hand to an independent artist, Robert Irwin. Comparisons of earlier schemes and the final project indicate a major shift from the unifying central garden concept of Meier's earlier designs to a literal rending

Fig. 4 Stone veneer as curtain wall.

Fig. 5 The garden designed by Robert Irwin literally splits the site between the museum and the research institute, interrupting one of the major organizational axis.

Fig. 6 Security guard stationed at the edge of Robert Irwin's garden design to prevent frustrated visitors from moving past the berm to gain access to the view and landscape beyond.

of the site between the Museum and the Research Institute. The result is a shifting of the dominant entrance axis from the garden to the museum. Rather than unification, the garden now emphasizes the differences between the Museum and the rest of the complex (fig. 5).

Meier further characterizes the Getty Center as "a place apart, yet firmly connected to the world beyond... is visible, accessible, and open to all."[11] Again, there is a fundamental contradiction in that the statement fails to confront the limitations of the initial site strategy and the institutional mandate. Getty Center is not a public park and in spite of its claims to have preserved and provided accessibility to a site that would have otherwise remained forever private, the sharing of the site with the public consists of mostly allowing for controlled views and overlook. Even the central garden is sectionally disconnected not only from the museum complex but also from views of the city. The museum plaza is elevated on a plinth two levels above the central garden, necessitating complicated ramp and stair connections. The garden is thus, also, separated from the entry plaza by the extension of this datum level forcing one to climb up and then descend to the garden. This procession is further limited by relying on a contrived zig-zag procession down the valley, flanked by the Museum on the east and the Research Institute on the west, to reach ultimately the central focus of the garden, a concentric circulation around a pool of floating flowers, focused inward and inaccessible to the view of the valley below (fig. 6). Meier contends that visitors "can explore the landscaping that covers most of the hill,"[12] but the actual experience is one of controlled movement and framed views rather than a sense of discovery. The analogy is more like a theme park ride, with a continuous pedestrian line moving down through the garden, than a great public garden. Recent visits to the museum have indicated that visitors are taking advantage of ambiguous gaps at the start of the proscribed circulation paths to the garden to break free and lounge on the gently sloping grass slopes that exist to mediate between the garden design and the museum. One can hopefully imagine the liberation of other portions of the site with similar results.

On my most recent "spontaneous" visit to the museum, prohibited from driving because of the two month lead time required for a reservation in the parking structure, I was dropped off in the perpetual traffic clog at the security gated entrance loop. From there I followed an uncharacteristically mean path between a wall and the bus parking accommodation to reach the top of the parking structure just as the tram left for the summit. It was late in the day on a Sunday and the traffic was mostly downhill, with an assortment of hearty souls trekking down the service road that parallels the rail route to the museum, rather than go through an extended wait in the tram queue at the top of the hill. From the tram platform, the view to the Center is artfully framed with an arched, shell roof. The tram trip is a six-minute ride to the summit. The route winding up the hill provides alternative vistas for the passengers, mostly tourists with a few local Angelenos, who point out city references and local flora to their guests on the tour. From the disembarkation plaza my attempt to ascend to the museum rotunda with projecting porte-cochere was dissuaded by the throngs of visitors descending on the stairway in a beeline to the tram queue. I took the path of least resistance, veered to the right and ascended a smaller stair, which adjusted my orientation to the axis of the central garden. This move was not really central in an operational sense, since the route I now followed is considerably below the datum level of the museum to the east and bordered on the west by the Research Institute. The Research Institute's enticing, curved, external terraces beckoned, but barriers with alarm warnings indicate that this part of the Getty is off limits. I must double-back to reach the restaurant and café building, which is suprisingly the only architectural element in the Complex that can be seen completely in the round. I stroll about this terrace, whose relationship to the entry plaza is cut off by a vehicular ramp connecting the plaza level with the museum datum level. Not only does this prevent the animation of the restaurant and cafe from spilling naturally out onto the plaza, the ramp is totally closed off to prevent any circulation except presumably in an emergency. This administrative overlay is a common experience in the complex, whose compositional axis is, all too often, interrupted with little signs in perfect Helvetica lettering indicating to the visitor that this or that portion of the Center is private with no access to the public. Meier, the master of articulated circulation, has been emasculated by the lack of fit between the formal vision and the functional necessities of an institution caught between the initial conception of a private enclave and the current reality of public consumption.

Alan Colquhoun, writing in *Essays in Architectural Criticism* about the museum as an instrument of culture, explains that the museum's responsibility can be understood as simultaneously addressing the belief that "on the one hand, culture is an innate endowment of each individual and on the other that it represents a set of values that must be taught."[13] The former position leads to a public driven architecture like Frank Gehry's Temporary Contemporary with its neutral typology allowing for multiple readings of context, adaptability, and creative overlays continuous with the urban fabric. The latter viewpoint is much more didactic, implying a conservative outlook in which the revolutionary positions of the past are converted into an orthodoxy, and the potential for change is seen as a threat to the established order. The Getty is caught in a paradox proposing change and growth in a closed system with an architecture that has its origins in creating the symbolism for a new social and cultural order. I trust the irony of this has not been lost on the institution.

1 Kevin Starr, Lecture at USC School of Architecture, October 28, 1998.

2 Harold M. Williams, "Introduction" in *Making Architecture: The Getty Center*, by Harold M. Williams, Ada L. Huxtable, Stephen D. Rountree, et. al. (Los Angeles: The J. Paul Getty Trust, 1997).

3 Heinrich Klotz and Waltraud Krase, *New Museum Buildings in the Republic of Germany* (New York: Rizzoli International Publications, 1985).

4 Stephen D. Rountree, "A Concert of Wills" in *Making Architecture: The Getty Center*, by Harold M. Williams, Ada L. Huxtable, Stephen D. Rountree, et. al. (Los Angeles: The J. Paul Getty Trust, 1997)

5 Richard Meier, "A Vision for Permanence" in *Making Architecture: The Getty Center*, by Harold M. Williams, Ada L. Huxtable, Stephen D. Rountree, et. al. (Los Angeles: The J. Paul Getty Trust, 1997)

6 *Ibid.*

7 *Ibid.*

8 Richard Meier, *Richard Meier, Architect: Buildings and Projects 1966-1976* (New York: Oxford University Press, 1976).

9 Robert Campbell, "A Critical Tour of the Getty," *Architectural Record* (November 1997), 106-116.

10 Meier, "A Vision for Permanence."

11 *Ibid.*

12 *Ibid.*

13 Alan Colquhoun, *Essays in Architectural Criticism: Modern Architecture and Historical Change* (Cambridge, Mass.: MIT Press, 1981).

Encore, Encore: Renovating Existing Structures for New Museum Spaces

Katrina Ampil Bagaybagayan

Museum of Contemporary Art, San Diego (La Jolla): An Essay in Architectural Historical Perspective

The Museum of Contemporary Art, San Diego (MCA), which began as a local art center in the small resort town of La Jolla, has metamorphosed into an internationally recognized and respected contemporary art museum, while still managing to retain its identification with the local community. MCA's colorful past is marked by its search for and validation of an identity in the contemporary art world. In 1983, Hugh Davies, MCA's director, proposed to the board of trustees that MCA undergo a major redesign and expansion to accommodate the museum's fast growth in programs, collection, and staff. In 1996, with its grand reopening on the original La Jolla site (fig. 2), redesigned by the architects Venturi, Scott Brown and Associates (VSBA), MCA finally achieved its goal of establishing a presence as the new power player on the contemporary art scene. Davies had an agenda for his new museum; he wanted to employ an architect whose work would attract critical attention and acclaim for the museum.[1] Inevitably, in the process of renovation and redesign, the architect and the client had to confront the inexorable history of the institution and the building. A review of MCA's history thus becomes an important gauge for estimating the interim stops and starts, the impediments and go-aheads, that determined VSBA's recreation of a working museum and the unadulterated realization of Davies's goal.

The original structure functioned not as a contemporary art museum but as a home for Miss Ellen Scripps, a newspaper heiress. Built in 1897 by local San Diego architects, it was destroyed by fire in 1915. Miss Scripps then commissioned a talented San Diegan architect, Irving Gill, to design her new house. Gill built in 1916 for Miss Scripps a modern house made of concrete and stucco.

Fig. 1 Exterior of the Museum of Contemporary Art, La Jolla.

In 1940, eight years after Scripps died, a group of artists took over the vacant building and used it as exhibition space. In 1941, the early ancestor of today's MCA was formally founded as the Art Center in La Jolla. It was a private, nonprofit organization, whose main purpose was to exhibit the art of local artists. Primarily intended as a home, the building's inappropriateness as an Art Center soon became apparent. In 1950, Robert Mosher and Roy Drew of the firm Mosher and Drew were commissioned to modify the building according to the needs of the emerging art institution. First floor living areas were retrofitted as galleries, storage spaces, classrooms, and a library. The bedrooms on the second floor became offices for the staff. Despite the extensive interior alterations, Mosher and Drew remained deferential to the beautiful simplicity of Gill's exterior design, including the distinctive arched façade.

As time passed, the Art Center outgrew its home again. In 1959, Mosher and Drew made further modifications and expansions to the structure. They added a new auditorium, a parking lot, a loading dock, and additional office spaces and exhibition galleries. In the process Gill's distinctive look disappeared, concealed by the new structural extensions of Mosher and Drew. The programs and collection increased in concert with the Art Center's physical growth. In 1964, its name was changed to La Jolla Museum of Art to better reflect its increased status. The museum began to find its niche in the art world when in the early 1970s a shift of focus from general art history to contemporary art took place.

In 1971, the board decided that henceforth, "The Museum will devote itself to Twentieth Century art with special emphasis on the art of today, including attention to the emerging artist.... At the same time, the Museum intends to achieve and maintain a significance and to perform an educational function that will have more than local importance."[2] Thus did the scope and goals of the museum expand once again, this time reaching beyond La Jolla to include the greater San Diego area in hopes of becoming an important art institution. To reflect this new focus, the museum underwent another name change to the La Jolla Museum of Contemporary Art. In 1980, Mosher and Drew were called in for the last time to modify the offices and galleries.

The arrival of Davies in 1983 as MCA's new director produced a fresh barrage of ideas about exhibition, acquisition, and education development. One of his first proposals was the renovation and expansion of MCA. Davies felt that the museum needed more exhibition space to enhance its ability to secure revenue, both from attendance and from donations. Most of all, Davies felt that MCA deserved "a building that took better advantage of its extraordinary site."[3]

Fig. 2 Façade.

Unanimously supported by the board in this renovation, Davies felt strongly that a well-known, highly reputable architect be chosen to redesign MCA. By having a famous and respected architect, MCA would inevitably attract critical attention and acclaim. The selection process was begun by an architectural committee who felt strongly that Gill's "precinct"—the group of Gill-designed buildings contiguous to MCA: Recreation Center, La Jolla Woman's Club, and Bishop's School—be included in whatever plans the architect might devise for MCA. Venturi, Scott Brown and Associates was selected, based upon its simultaneous (seemingly contradictory) appreciation of the Gill environs and ambition to propel the building's overall design into the twentieth century (fig. 3).

Fig. 3 MCA, as viewed through the arches of the Woman's Club.

VSBA accepted the MCA commission, because, among other reasons, it would allow the architects to explore Gill's Modernist designs. Venturi's interest in history and vernacular architecture is evident in his earliest work, a house for Vanna Venturi, his mother. This house, with its exaggerated features of a huge pitched roof, an oversized front door, and an extra large chimney, is indicative of Venturi's fascination with mannerist and, on the contrary, grass-roots architecture. The Post-Modernist firm of VSBA had been influenced by the vernacular architecture of the English architect Sir Edwin Lutyens, who always inserted into his design and construction of homes in the late nineteenth and early twentieth centuries, a strange twist, an exaggeration or a mixing of stylistic elements that produced contradictions and complexities in an otherwise indigenous structure. Gill's Scripps House, with its mixture of Modernist and Arts and Crafts style, reminiscent of some of Lutyens's homes, was the ideal vehicle for VSBA's confrontation of history in its architectural style. For VSBA the commission to redesign MCA was an opportunity to demonstrate just how important tradition figures in its architecture. The decisions that VSBA made regarding what Gill design elements were to be brought back and what late twentieth-century design tunes it would play as variations on the building adumbrate the Post-Modernist ideals of this firm. VSBA had to create a structure that would simultaneously accommodate a complex museum program and establish MCA's identity as an institution of civic importance. It is through architectural scale that VSBA has evoked the civic identity. Although MCA comprises a moderately small building (from the street the museum is seemingly only one story tall), the architectural features taken from Gill's buildings (the arch, the column, and the columned pergolas) have been exaggerated in size to create a sense of the civic function and importance of the institution. Unfortunately, the scale of these features differentiate the museum from

Fig. 4 Edwards Garden, with Gabriel Orozco's installation, Long Yellow Hose *(1996).*

the rest of Gill's precinct. MCA's doric columns are short and thick and dwarf the domestic-sized columns of the Woman's Club. Unlike the surrounding Gill buildings, which recess from the sidewalk, MCA is positioned against the curb. This factor influenced VSBA in its introduction of new design features, which ultimately put its characteristic stamp on the project. One innovation was a sidewalk cafe. Neon signs locate it, as well as the auditorium, ticket office, and bookstore, as additions borrowed from the contemporary world of advertising. The glare of the neon lights at night further contradicts the simple and clean aesthetic of the Gill-inspired design. VSBA has also added a subtle yet distinctively Venturi design component in the columned pergolas and large entrance arch. From across the street it appears to be the main entrance to the museum. Yet as one approaches this putative entrance one is surprised to discover that it is a faux entrance, and one must veer left to enter the museum through a door not initially visible. Thus does VSBA idiosyncratically, and perversely, challenge and confound the viewer in the liberties it has taken with Gill's design.

The relationship between architect and client is an important factor in the success of a museum's design and construction. The genial collaboration of Davies and VSBA was so ideal that when Davies was asked to comment on how he felt about the redesign he answered that he would change nothing.[4] Indeed, critics have accused the museum of letting VSBA have a complete run of the place, and, as a result, allowing it to produce an architectural statement that reduces the art inside to a whisper. It is true that Davies and the museum seem to have struck a Faustian bargain with VSBA.[5] There was, however, one caveat. Although the architects were given free reign in the design of the exterior and the entrance hall, the museum insisted that the galleries remain decoratively neutral.

Venturi, Scott Brown and Associates accordingly allowed for subdued white walls, and for transitory spaces between galleries to give the viewer an opportunity to take a breather. In these secondary areas, one is afforded sights of the garden and the Pacific Ocean (fig. 4). VSBA likens this to a theatrical experience, where the space becomes magical, because, in part, of its shifting contrast between the aesthetic ambiance of the art galleries and the realistic vistas of the outside world.[6] VSBA has nevertheless left its trademark signature of challenge on the layout of the galleries (fig. 5). Like a maze, the galleries offer neither a sense of direction nor a clear-cut traffic pattern for the visitor. The varying perspectives of the Pacific Ocean also can disorient viewers' sense of direction as they thread their way, tracking and backtracking, through an exhibition.

The one part of the interior where Venturi had carte blanche to indulge his design theories was the entrance hall, named Axline Court (fig. 6). Here VSBA indulges in a bit of architectural fanfare to call attention to the museum's function as a civic building.[7] In contrast to the

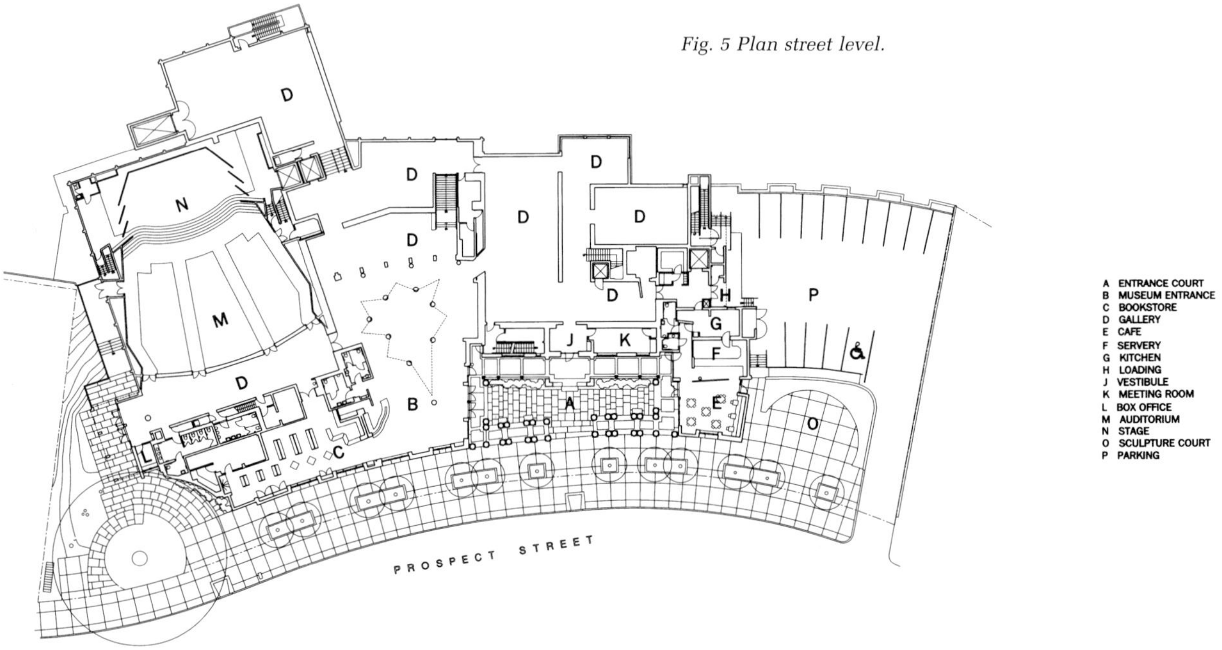

Fig. 5 Plan street level.

restrained responsibility with which Venturi deals with the Prospect Street façade vis-à-vis Gill's precinct and with the interior galleries of neutral white, Axline Court's starburst shaped ceiling—not apparent from the outside—hits the viewer with a shock of surprise. Soaring overhead is a sunken dome in the form of a seven-pointed star with neon fitted fins. On the floor are matching patterns of "dalmatian" or terrazzo spots. The downside of this architectural spectacle is that the visitor's sense of direction in the galleries is compounded by the layout of Axline Court providing four entrances into the viewing areas from which to choose.

Fig. 6 Axline Court, with Sol Lewitt's Isometric Pyramid *(1983).*

On the plus side, the architects have redesigned the museum with its history in mind, while making decisions internally and externally that reflect their perceptions of what a contemporary art museum should look like. Its historical metamorphoses have left layers of reference that VSBA and client have used as a context for giving MCA a visual identity. The external façade reflects an architectural effort to identify MCA with local community history and the original Gill precinct, without compromising VSBA's Post-Modernist principles. The eastern face confronts the cityscape of La Jolla and establishes the museum's civic relationship with the town. The western side overlooks the Pacific Ocean, which contributes to the backyard feeling of the garden's design.

Although architectural reviews and articles about VSBA's design were mixed, the attention MCA has attracted from the museum and architectural worlds would seem to have justified its hiring of a world-famous architect. MCA's journey through multiple identities has been long and arduous. The newly redesigned building is one that is tied to its history and roots but which also looks ahead to the twenty-first century.

1 Hugh Davies, interview by author, La Jolla, CA, 12 March 1998.
2 Trustee Policy, La Jolla Museum of Contemporary Art, revised 21 December, 1971.
3 Hugh Davies and Anne Farrell, *Learning from La Jolla* (San Diego, CA: Museum of Contemporary Art, San Diego, 1996), 21.
4 Hugh Davies, interview by author, La Jolla, CA, 12 March 1998.
5 *Ibid.*
6 Davies and Farrell, 39.
7 *Ibid.*, 39.

Karen Weldon Roswell

The Temporary Contemporary: The Warehouse That Could

Viewed from a panoptic perspective, MOCA was always a project designed to change the nature of perception about Los Angeles.[1]

The changing role of art museums in society, from isolated repositories of aesthetic heritage to experientially driven destinations of culture and entertainment, has had tremendous repercussions on the physical design and layout of new museum spaces built in the last twenty-five years of this century. Whether constructing an entirely new site, or refurbishing with an eye toward achieving contemporary stature and parity with other cultural venues, art museums have increasingly sought out the services of star architects to create singular architectural masterpieces that command attention and attract visitors. The modern idea that museum architecture should be a creative focal point in itself, rather than serving as a neutral backdrop for the display of valued works of art, has been hyper-realized by the pressing need to entice patrons and donors to support these institutions. Consequently, signature buildings have become paramount, with the result that form all too often eclipses function, and the physical structure overshadows the art it is built to showcase. In a world where media coverage dictates tastes and trends that transcend international boundaries, this contradiction is further complicated when cities seek to erect museums that will serve as consummate visual symbols, indeed, urban monuments, of their cultural significance. In this context, an art museum's strong architectural imagery becomes a manifesto in and of itself.

Fig. 1 Aerial view of Central Avenue and surrounding environs. Temporary Contemporary warehouses visible, upper right side.

Yet, not every art museum that seeks to make a cultural statement has to be a monument. Art museums that manage to realize successful interior exhibition spaces, regardless of exterior appearances, can communicate a cultural message as potent as any architectural tour de force that upstages the significance of its acquisitions. Achieving a balance between the architectural envelope and the art it con-

Fig. 2 The warehouse interior, used as a police car repair garage (1981).

tains is especially important for museums exhibiting the work of living artists. Structures that allow artists the latitude to experiment—rather than forcing them to subordinate their work to limited spatial contexts—can serve as catalysts for new forms of artistic expression. The Temporary Contemporary annex (recently renamed the Geffen Contemporary) to the Museum of Contemporary Art (MOCA) on Bunker Hill in downtown Los Angeles is a case in point. Located in two warehouses—combined and refurbished—on a cul-de-sac in Little Tokyo, the Temporary's fifty-five thousand square feet of exhibition space has enabled it to pursue diverse and unconventional programming and garnered it an international reputation as one of the most innovative venues of contemporary art. This recycled building was never conceived of as a self-reflective civic emblem, yet it shares the spotlight with some of the world's most renowned art museums, in part because its humble beginnings offer a contrast to the prevailing aesthetic of spectacle. The subtlety of the Temporary's transformation exemplifies a unique institutional symbiosis of form and function that energizes the imagination of artist and viewer alike by continuing to keep pace with the changing demands of ever more ambitious, large, and complex art objects, mixed media, and installation/performance pieces.

As an inspired response to the city's immediate need for a facility to showcase contemporary art, the Temporary Contemporary opened in 1983 as an interim exhibition space while the permanent location of the fledgling MOCA was under construction. MOCA's landmark building designed by Arata Isozaki was an important item on Mayor Tom Bradley's ambitious agenda in presenting Los Angeles as a "world city,"[2] and was originally scheduled for completion in time for the city to host the 1984 Olympic Games. As it became evident that this deadline could not be met, Richard Koshalek, the museum's director, realized that the long and arduous process of getting the project underway threatened to derail civic and public confidence in the museum during its early days. Koshalek and his staff initially considered the idea of a "guerrilla museum," protean programming presented to the public in undeveloped and neglected urban spaces such as vacant lots and abandoned buildings.[3] But as the timeline for completion of MOCA continued to be extended, the concept of a "temporary contemporary" seemed to best suit the museum's need for securing its image within the community and establishing a presence in time for the Olympic Games.

Frank Gehry was given the commission of renovating the two empty shells of wall and roof, which had once served as a hardware factory and police car repair garage (fig. 2). Gehry was not selected for his "starchitect"[4] power and prestige; his international reputation had yet to be established. Although Gehry had a unique opportunity to put MOCA on the cultural map, as it were, he also faced two challenges—the museum's need for exhibition space was urgent and the budget was limited to approximately $1.5 million. Undaunted, Gehry focused on creating a highly functional and engaging space. Understanding that the combined structure would showcase the work of living artists, Gehry was sensitive to the methods and workspaces of contemporary artistic production. The raw qualities of the two buildings appealed to his architectural aesthetic and to his artist's instincts, so he set out to renovate them with minimal intervention. As Gehry noted at the time:

> *Some architects might have been inclined to redo the space—I was inclined not to. I guess my inspiration for this is the artists themselves, who, when they buy or rent old commercial spaces, just clean them up and put their work in—and the places are beautiful. So I've taken my cue from this and tried not to* DE-sign *it.*[5]

Fig. 3 Interior wall construction.

Fig. 4 Exterior canopy.

In six months, Gehry subtly transformed the vast warehouse interiors into an unencumbered and elastic space. He took care to preserve the exposed structural steel beams, steam-cleaned the twenty-eight-foot-high redwood ceilings and illuminated them with track lighting, reglazed the skylights and clerestory windows, and installed large plate glass window-and-door entrances (fig. 3). The cumulative effect of these and other minor changes brought the building up to code and enlivened it with an easy, loft-like atmosphere. Gehry's only personal addition was a chain-link-mesh canopy that stretches from the entrance of the building across the entire street in front of the structure, reflecting his concern about preserving the "street roots" of the museum as other buildings surrounding the warehouse were torn down (fig. 4).

The renovation met with much acclaim—the local press hailed it as a resourceful and elegant exhibition space. William Wilson, an art critic for the *Los Angeles Times*, wrote of the Temporary when it first opened:

> *A prominent visiting East Coast critic echoed what appears to be a consensus reaction to the gallery: "now that you have this, why would you ever want to move upon the hill?" As a building, Temporary Contemporary seems to have it all: a copious and highly flexible space, impressive enough to enhance anything that goes in it; a picturesque aura of do-it-ourselves Post-Modernist recycling that inspires empathetic admiration.*[6]

Reconditioning the derelict buildings also seemed to embody the free spirit of Southern California. As one critic has noted:

> *The T.C. [Temporary Contemporary] looks like a distillation of Southern California's vernacular architecture, creating poetry, drama, and public engagement from the commonplace, the unsurprising, and the unfinished. As such, the T.C. building became the local art community's symbol, which would arouse from the freeways, fast-food restaurants, blue skies and tract houses, a contemporary art that would differ from the Modern as the Modern had differed from salon art of the 19th-century.*[7]

Seen in this light, the warehouse stands as a manifesto of Los Angeles's discrete urban and cultural landscape.

MOCA at the Temporary was an immediate success. Within two months after opening, the museum had ten thousand members,[8] even though the permanent Bunker Hill site was still three years from completion. When the doors to MOCA finally opened in 1986, the museum made the decision to keep the Little Tokyo understudy as an annex to its new facility. More than just an improvisational venue, the Temporary had come to signify MOCA's commitment to seeking a forum for the exchange, and public presentation, of artistic ideas. It was an experimental workspace that demystified the making of art and secularized its sacrosanct place of display.

Free from the shadow of signature design, the Temporary's cavernous interior has been reconfigured over the years in any number of ways to meet the needs of artists and curators. Indeed, many collaborative and multidisciplinary projects have depended on the Temporary's ability to transform itself. In 1986, a multi-media exhibition of Jonathan Borofsky's work included a basketball court—on which the public was invited to play—in addition to paintings, drawings, sculpture, video, and music. For the 1989 architectural exhibition, "Blueprints for Modern Living: History and Legacy of the Case Study Houses," the Temporary "housed" two full-scale reconstructions of original Case Study homes, which provided the contextual backdrop to a retrospective of Modern architecture in the postwar era. The 1995 residency exhibition, "Action Occupation," found New York-based movement artist Elizabeth Streb and her company Ringside crashing through plate glass walls and bouncing off spring-loaded floors. As one of six group projects featured in "Uncommon Sense," a 1997 show focused on exploring social interaction with art in unusual situations, artists Ann Carlson and Mary Ellen Strom installed a rodeo arena complete with a live horse (fig. 5). This same exhibition also prominently displayed a replica of the set from the television series "Melrose Place," and an MTA bus in which the Cornerstone Theater Company performed several one-act plays. In his first solo exhibition in the United States, sculptor Robert Gober created a site-specific installation that required water to flow across the floor and into holes dug into the foundation that revealed subterranean tidepools. For the 1998 Richard Serra show a 30' x 30' section of one wall was removed so that a number of Serra's colossal sculptural works—usually seen out of doors in isolation from one another—could be brought together inside the museum (fig. 6). All of these examples are a testament to the flexibility of the Temporary's programming; by making the space accessible to artists the facility is continually redefining the museum experience from the inside out.

Fig. 5 Rodeo performance by Ann Carlson and Mary Ellen Strom, presented as part of "Uncommon Sense" (1997).

Philosophically, MOCA at the Temporary can trace its roots to two experiments in the public presentation of art, P.S. 1 in Long

Island City and the Centre Pompidou in Paris. During the 1960s and 1970s, the efforts of individual artists to create venues in which to showcase their work outside the rigid institutional confines of traditional museums led to the proliferation of alternative spaces in vacant urban buildings, of which P.S. 1 is an example. Located in an abandoned turn-of-the century public school, P.S. 1 began in 1976 as an experimental gallery where artists lived, worked, and exhibited. Over the past twenty-two years, the building has been gradually renovated to become a perma-

Fig. 6 Torqued Ellipse IV *by Richard Serra (1998). Dimensions: 12'3" x 26'6" x 32'6", approximate overall weight: 80,000 lbs.*

nent facility dedicated to exploring the broad range of creative endeavors that define contemporary art.[9] As an extension of the movement to achieve greater interaction between artists and their audience, the Centre Pompidou was one of the first museums that sought to replicate—on an institutional level—the "non-style of alternative space"[10] that artists prized so in the industrial buildings they converted into studios. Completed in 1977 as the cultural focal point in an urban renewal project, the Paris museum was intended to facilitate a more democratic rapport between artists and the public by facilitating a disparate array of interdisciplinary exhibitions. Although the immense interior, with its exposed ceiling ducts and support fixtures, was designed to promote an atmosphere of artistic freedom similar to that in the "found" workspace of an artist's loft, the Centre Pompidou's "non-style" was the deliberate creation of architects producing a landmark building. The Temporary synthesizes elements of both of these trail-blazing museums: capturing the spontaneity of a recycled, alternative venue within the organizational framework of a museum. The resulting measure of "institutional" freedom has enabled MOCA's secondary facility to stimulate the cultural pulse of downtown Los Angeles since its inception.

The Temporary is a place of unlimited potential. As such, the venue is an ongoing work in progress. Its soul is embodied in the alignment of form and function, manifested by its continued willingness to literally transform itself (and in some cases deface itself) in the interest of programmatic integrity. The building has received international acclaim not simply for the brilliance of Gehry's renovation but because of its ability to reinvent itself as needed. Though other contemporary art museums have successfully imitated the raw quality of Gehry's renovation, they have done so with new buildings or with annexed commercial structures as secondary facilities. The adventurous spirit and unique conditions of the Temporary have proven difficult to capture; in this respect, MOCA's readiness to risk establishing its presence in a provisional location cannot be discounted. The fact that the Temporary had such an inauspicious beginning actually endeared it to the art-going public immediately, and conferred upon it landmark status long before MOCA's permanent home was completed. The combined warehouse was situated at the right place, at the right time, in the right city. Its metamorphosis from an undecorated shed to an undecorated tour de force communicates a message of ingenuity that cannot be replicated simply by copying its brick and mortar.

Will this success eventually be its undoing? One hopes not, yet there are disturbing signs. Though MOCA does not actively seek to cultivate different identities or audiences for the two sites—it is promoted as "one museum, two buildings"—changes are taking place that may firmly institutionalize the status of the museum's alternative space. In 1996, through a generous gift of $5 million from entertainment impresario David Geffen, the name was changed from the Temporary Contemporary to the Geffen Contemporary. The investment of an "official" name was the subject of much debate within the Los Angeles art community; the term "temporary" did not merely describe a once provisional venue, it had become equated with a sense of urban spontaneity. But now we know the Temporary is no longer just that. Augmenting its name change are pending renovations (initiated during Koshalek's tenure as director), which are slated to include a Digital Art Center, a coffee bar, and a sculptural signage piece. As if brought back by popular demand, Gehry has been designated to perform once again his architectural conjuration, this time in the location under the chain link canopy that he designed at the entrance to the building in 1983. While such attractions may dress up the exterior and, by proximity, apply a signature to the otherwise anonymous exterior, it is heartening that the integrity of the unassuming "found" space will presumably remain intact. Hopefully the symbiotic balance of form and function will continue to present itself as a work in progress, a contemporary Kunsthalle with the power to capture and vitalize the creative spirit.

1 Jo-Anne Berelowitz, "The Museum of Contemporary Art, Los Angeles: An Account of Collaboration Between Artists, Trustees and an Architect," in *Art Apart: Art Institutions and Ideology Across England and North America*, ed. Marcia Pointon (New York, Manchester: Manchester University Press, 1994), 274.

2 Berelowitz, 268.

3 Patricia Failing, "MOCA: Los Angeles Gets its Long-awaited Museum of Contemporary Art—or at Least a Temporary Contemporary," *ARTNews* 82 (October 1983): 107.

4 Reesa Greenberg, "The Exhibited Redistributed: A Case for Reassessing Space," in *Thinking About Exhibitions*, ed. Reesa Greenberg, Bruce W. Ferguson, and Sandy Nairne (London: Routledge, 1996), 362.

5 Failing, 107.

6 William Wilson, "Temporary Contemporary: Its Time is Now," *Los Angeles Times*, 20 November 1983, sec. C.

7 Herbert Muschamp, "The L.A. Museum of Contemporary Art: What's in a Name?" *Architectural Record* 175 (May 1987): 85.

8 Pilar Viladas, "The Undecorated Shed," *Progressive Architecture* (March 1984): 84.

9 Douglas Davis, *The Museum Transformed* (New York: Abbeville Press Publishers, 1990), 177.

10 The recent merger between P. S. 1 and the Museum of Modern Art (MOMA) in New York will officially institutionalize the old school house, providing MOMA with much-need exhibition space as well as a connection to the world of contemporary art.

Claudia A. Leos

The Museum of Contemporary Art, San Diego (Downtown): The Socialization of Museum Design

Museum architecture has traditionally reflected its origins in royal and aristocratic collections. Early museums emulated the grand mansions and imperial palaces of princes, using arched entries, noble pillars, and long courtyards, to symbolize the museum's importance, as, for example, characterizes Karl Friedrich Schinkel's Altes Museum, Berlin, of 1830. When possible, museums even inhabited converted royal structures, a key instance of worldwide fame being the postrevolutionary Louvre. The stately monuments built according to this tradition formally signaled to the public that the museum was a treasure house, a revered place, which enclosed and sanctified art. Inviting to the learned elite, intimidating to the general public, the so-called architecture of the palace, of Kunsthallen and picture galleries, became the standard in nineteenth- and early twentieth-century museum building in Europe and America, despite the museum's growing didactic and democratic functions. American examples include the Metropolitan Museum in New York, the Museum of Fine Arts in Boston, the National Gallery of Art in Washington D.C., and the Henry E. Huntington Library and Art Gallery in San Marino, California.

Since the mid-twentieth century, however, many museums have rebelled against this dictum, opting for an architecture that departs from traditional exteriors and conventional gallery layouts. In 1960, the spiral gallery walkway of Frank Lloyd Wright's Guggenheim Museum gave revolutionary impetus to the redesign of art palaces. A classless definition of the museum was heralded in the late 1970s with Renzo Piano and Richard Rogers's Centre Pompidou in Paris. This futuristic steel and glass structure with servicing ducts and boxes, and huge outdoor escalators exposed on the façade, broke new ground in the socialization of museum design. There was no formal entry; the galleries were not rooms but large, open, and flexible spaces to be shaped by the curatorial staff as they wished. It also contained not only art, but a library, cinemas, restaurants, and cafes.

Fig. 1 South plaza of the Museum of Contemporary Art, (Downtown), at night.

Fig. 2 South plaza, trolley station.

In the aptly titled book, *The Museum Transformed*, Douglas Davis argues for the Centre Pompidou's significance to later museum architecture:

> *The Pompidou Center became a turning point in the design of museums by stating the case for the desanctification of art—for the museum as a container of "culture" in the broad, vulgar sense—with such force that it could not be ignored. After Pompidou the museum community and its architects were either forced to reject this standard or accept its implications.*[1]

Crucial to this new attitude vis-à-vis museum architecture is that the museum has grown more sensitive about its role as a civic institution bent on courting a mass public in addition to the elite of previous centuries. The idea of the museum as a treasure trove of precious objects was countered by postmodern[2] thinking. Its questioning the authority of the art object contributed to a new view of the museum as a "complex phenomenon, where temporal events and activities swirl around and beyond the viewing of treasures."[3] The response of Michael Graves to critics of his expansion of the Whitney Museum in 1986 epitomizes this change in architecture and in function:

> *I think this is a moment in history where we have to realize that we're not just building Kunsthallen.... We're building institutions that have places for discussion, places for study, and a* ***social*** *climate as well as a climate in which to see painting and sculpture.*[4] *(Emphasis added.)*

The Museum of Contemporary Art, San Diego, Downtown (MCA Downtown), which opened in 1993, corresponds to the late twentieth-century anti-palace, non-monument, school of museum design (fig. 1). The modest exterior, minimalist interior, nonaxis-based asymmetrical rooms, natural light from large and small windows, as well as the urban and mass transit surroundings, declare its non-adherence to the museum typology of the intimidating palace or treasure house. These features intentionally constitute a populist and social space for viewing art and for mounting cultural programs like dance, poetry, and art workshops that are welcoming to the city's diverse population. In fact, attracting a broad-based audience was a principal social goal in the decision of the Museum of Contemporary Art (based in the San Diego community of La Jolla) to add a branch in downtown San Diego.[5]

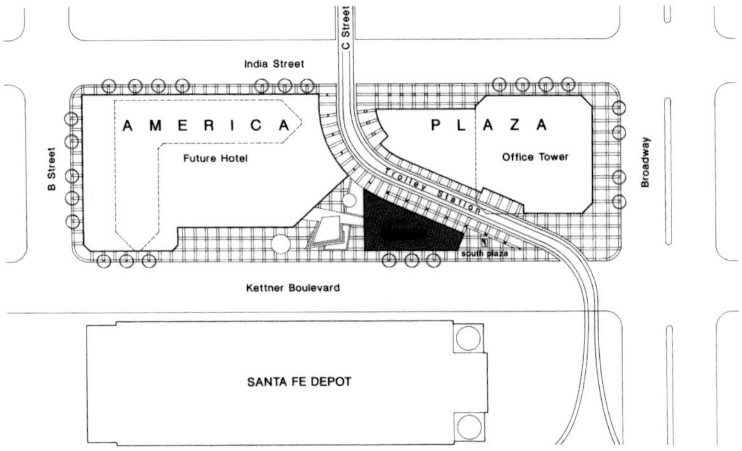

Fig. 3 Site plan: museum in black.

With the arrival of a new director, Hugh Davies, in 1983, MCA San Diego, then known as the La Jolla Museum of Contemporary Art, underwent a critical review of its institutional identity.[6] Its name change to a more encompassing moniker coincided with its new policy of addressing the whole San Diego/Tijuana region with community outreach programs, bilingual materials, and Latino and "Border" art exhibitions.[7] MCA envisioned an urban downtown site—as counterpoint to its idyllic beachfront museum in La Jolla—one that would engage the whole population of the city.[8] In particular, MCA targeted the Latino audience in recognition of the strong bicultural makeup of the area—Latinos being the fastest growing segment demographically—and the importance of focusing on the border region of California and Mexico.[9]

The site and shape of the museum is ideal for its accessibility to a broader audience than is possible for the wealthy enclave of La Jolla, a beach resort located fifteen miles north of downtown San Diego. MCA Downtown is centrally situated at the hub of the city's mass transit. The building is actually attached to the trolley transfer station (fig. 2), which was built as part of the two-block America Plaza complex, designed by Helmut Jahn of Murphy/Jahn, Chicago. Its east side acts as a waiting curb for trolley passengers. The San Diego Trolley consists of a two-line system that converges at the America Plaza transfer station, next to the museum (fig. 3). The trolley's route reaches as far east as El Cajon and Santee, north to the historic Mission San Diego in Mission Valley, and all the way south to San Ysidro/Tijuana. The trolley system particularly serves the Latino and African-American communities, which are concentrated in the east and south county areas. Its west side and museum entrance face the historic Santa Fe depot. There, Amtrak and Coaster trains arrive hourly from the north. The nearby popular Gaslamp Quarter houses shops, restaurants, and nightclubs, which fill day and night with tourists and San Diegans from all over the county.

Although the museum and its design team were initially offered space on the ground floor of a yet-to-be-built hotel at America Plaza, they chose the wedge-shaped, trolley transfer structure (intended for retail use) that was nearly completed.[10] The design team put together by director Davies consisted of two artists, Robert Irwin and David Fleischner, and local architect David R. Singer. Judging the building a "far better museum space," than the proposed space, the designers had the idea of function in mind from the

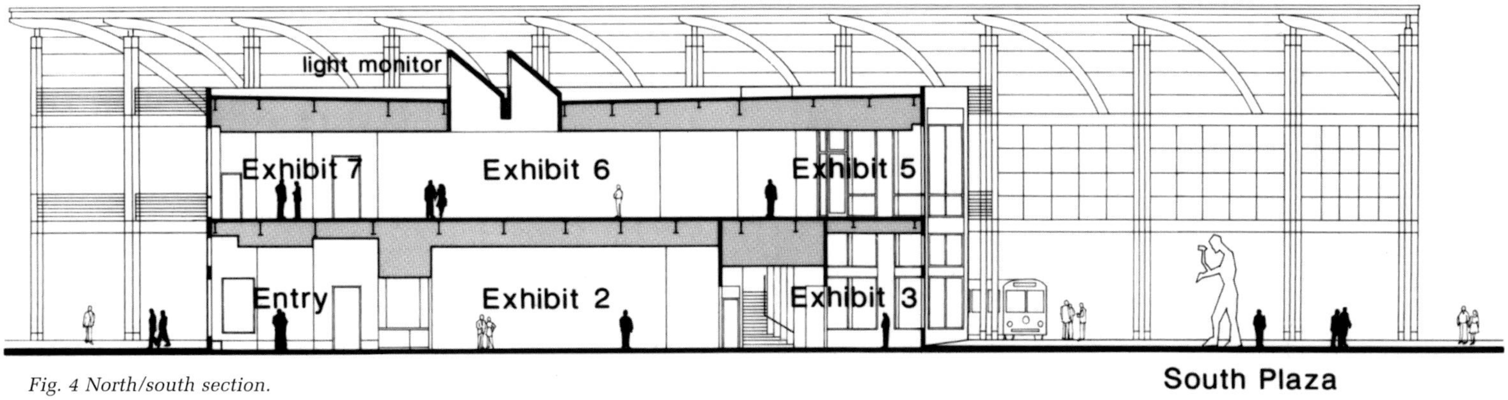

Fig. 4 North/south section.

very beginning, stating that they "wanted to best serve the art and the [future] exhibitions."[11] In a 1992 interview about the new museum building, Irwin commented that museums usually "go wrong" when they try to implement grandiose intentions: "Museums are inclined to build monuments, cities want this too. Why build a hard-working art museum, the argument goes, when you can have a culturally identifiable monument." His colleague Fleischner then added, "We were more interested in how it could function, than [in] the container."[12]

The exterior of the building is a glass and steel envelope with gray granite facing. The details inherent in the architecture of the palace or museum-as-treasure-house are missing here. There is no formal entry arch, no stepped ramp, no grand forecourt leading into the building. It is at street level, very much part of the public walkway, and negligibly distant from the thoroughfare and trolley tracks. The north-west entry, a pair of simple glass doors opening to the exhibition rooms, is actually so discreet that it takes a moment to find when approached from the south-east trolley side, where the bookstore's entrance is located. MCA's situation at the crossroads of transportation for the county makes it unconventionally accessible for a museum and, moreover, symbolizes the museum's populist and inclusionary attitude. It presents such a true alternative to the dichotomy of the La Jolla site, which is located in an affluent and insular area that is difficult to reach by public transportation.

The building itself rejects the traditional axis of museum design, an enfilade of rooms surrounding the central axis of a courtyard or rotunda. Rather, after entering the two-story edifice, one proceeds through both large and small asymmetrical rooms on each floor. The major spaces are left unpartitioned, flexible and open, so that they may be converted into smaller rooms, depending on the special requirements for exhibitions of contemporary artwork, particularly video and site installations. For example, a small screening room (on the first floor) was created in the large gallery for William Kentridge's video installation last year.

The dimensions of the galleries were inherently odd because of the wedge-shaped exterior shell, but instead of chopping them up into the typical square or rectangle by building interior walls at right angles—and thereby wasting space—the design team allowed the inner wall to echo the outer, creating unconventional gallery spaces and gaining maximum wall space for exhibitions. Since the façades were principally glass-curtains, the windows had to be blocked on the interior with walls along the length of the west and east street sides. To avoid showing a blank face to the street, Irwin—true to his light and space orientation—devised an opaque paint pattern for the windows, which throws lively shadows on the inner walls.

Glass, opening up the museum to the neighborhood, and vice versa giving the neighborhood visibility, is a prominent architectural feature of the MCA downtown site: the large showcase windows, the glazing treatment, the interior "connecting" windows, all give the space "added light, activity, and orientation,"[14] contributing to a sense of interactiveness that breaks with the tradition of museums as static, sanctimonious, and insular environments. At the north and south ends, as a public extension of the galleries, floor to ceiling windows on both levels overlook open air plazas displaying public art, usually large sculpture (fig. 4 and 5). The south end galleries act as showcases to the populace at large, since passersby can eye the art exhibited in them; contrariwise, museum visitors can glimpse dynamic blurs of moving cherry red trolleys and intriguing, fragmented views of the city and bay beyond.[13] The north end contains the entry lobby, orientation/reading space for visitors and groups, and bookstore. The latter for structural reasons remains unconnected to the lobby,[15] but is linked visually by way of glass walls, allowing views into the bookstore from the orientation space, the stairway corridor, the garage elevator lobby, and the lobby reception desk. The elevation is actually three feet higher on the bookstore's west side and these windows exploit this fact, making visual the "street" drama of museumgoers.

Fig. 5 Museum and people at trolley station.

The interior decor is kept simple. Walls are painted white within the galleries. Floors are oak in the lobby and orientation space but concrete inside the galleries. The exhibition spaces have a rugged loft-style feel, similar to the studios where much contemporary art is created. In their understatement they are neither distracting to the art nor intimidating to first-time museumgoers. Even the large skylight that allows natural lighting on the second level is discreetly tucked into the ceiling.

Fig. 6 Façade of the San Diego Museum of Art.

This small museum with its low-key architecture and humble location in the midst of mass transit has succeeded in helping MCA broaden its audience. The building, in its appearance and placement, is a sign of the more inclusive attitude about art for the masses that has been adopted by MCA. Prior to the downtown site the museum's membership came mainly from La Jolla and the neighboring coastal communities of Pacific Beach and Del Mar. Today that demographic area constitutes one-third of the thirty-one hundred members, and the area outside of it, the rest of San Diego county, makes up the remaining two-thirds.[16] The attendance at Sunday "free-for-all" family workshops, a "high-profile program of community activities, many of them targeted to Latino families," has reached two hundred visitors downtown,[17] approaching the La Jolla location's three hundred visitors.[18] The Latino audience represents at least twenty-five percent of the total attendance at the Sunday events, which, according to the museum's community outreach coordinator, Gwendolyn Gomez, is more than triple their usual Latino audience.[19]

For MCA downtown the collaborative design team chose an extant building and shaped it into an unpretentious space that is minimalist and self-effacing vis-à-vis the art and the people who enter or look in from the outside. Bravo! for MCA's championship of that philosophy in its downtown San Diego site. The museum has succeeded in creating the social climate that Graves spoke of when he was creating the Whitney Museum extension. It offers a dynamic meeting place for the public, whether they enter for an exhibition or special program or just enjoy the public art in the plazas and shop at the bookstore while waiting for the trolley (fig. 5).

The architecture of the anti-palace and its freer interpretation of museum design has succeded in this case. MCA Downtown presents a suitable environment for both the art and the community who visit it, an accessible, urban-integrated space that does not seem overpowering or imposing to its audience. This kind of architecture departs from the strict formality of earlier museums, such as the grand Spanish Colonial revivals in San Diego's Balboa Park complex, featuring palatial entries and ennobling fronts (fig. 6). It suits the heterogeneous nature of contemporary art as well as of contemporary urban audiences.

Once again, bravo for the populist and comfortable environment MCA Downtown facilitates, which has helped this particular museum realize its admirable and farsighted goals for a changing America at the end of the twentieth century.

1 Douglas Davis, *The Museum Transformed* (New York: Abbeville Press Publisher, 1990), 42.

2 Postmodern is used here in its sense as a term of literary and art critical theory rather than of architectural practice.

3 Davis, 30.

4 *Ibid.*, 32.

5 Robert L. Pincus, "A Contemporary Move: Museum Hopes Converts Will Find Open Doors," *San Diego Union Tribune*, 7 February 1993, sec. E, p.1.

6 Gwendolyn Gomez and Anne Farrell, "From Theory to Practice: Developing Diversity, Three Case Studies," *Museum News* (May/June 1998): 53.

7 *Ibid.*

8 Preston Turegano, "Museum is Moving Ahead With Another Name, Another Space," *San Diego Union Tribune*, 7 February 1993, E2.

9 Gomez and Farrell, 53.

10 Robert L. Pincus, "Artists Helped Shape New Museum," *San Diego Union Tribune*, 29 April 1992, D9.

11 Diane Maxwell, "Museum of Contemporary Art, San Diego: The New Downtown Building." Museum of Contemporary Art, San Diego News Release, 10 December 1992.

12 Pincus, "Artists Helped Shape New Museum," D9.

13 Leah Ollman, "A Trolley's Eye View," *Art News* 92 (September 1993): 26.

14 Ann Jarmusch, "A Contemporary Move: La Jolla Institution Discovers Life Downtown," *San Diego Union Tribune*, 7 February 1993, sec. E, p. 1.

15 Hugh Davies, interview by author, La Jolla, CA, 11 March 1998.

16 Davies, interview.

17 Gomez and Farrell, 53.

18 Davies, interview.

19 Gomez and Farrell, 54.

Susan Camille Passow

Phoenix Art Museum: A Civic Symbol in Progress

A new museum for the new century contributes to the transformation of this desert city's self image.[1]

In the midst of the Sonoran Desert lies a meticulous configuration of municipalities paradoxically termed Paradise Valley. An unwelcome reminder of human domination encroaching upon the serene beauty of the desert, it is a decentralized matrix of unvaried city planning that seems to expand indefinitely. Beyond, the vista reveals mile after mile of variations on the color brown: the buff color of the sandy panorama, the rusty brown of the rock formations, the setaceous vegetation sprouting from the tan, barren landscape. The heat strikes with a solidity that is almost painful. For all the careful structuring of the grid, the area seems like a part of the world that has been forgotten, a frontier town that has been abandoned by temporary inhabitants who have gone on to the more hospitable, arable West Coast.

Such an impression, though easy to form, would be deceptive. In actuality, Phoenix is a thriving metropolis that has until recently managed to maintain a small town demeanor. Comprised of nineteen contiguous communities, it is ranked as the seventh largest city in the United States.[2] Warm weather year-round, and abundant, readily available land awaiting the civilizing grid, has caused the population to grow from one hundred thousand to more than two million in just forty years.[3] The parched desert is dotted with lush golf courses flourishing in the burning sun—thanks to irrigation and allocated city water, without any apprehension regarding possible future consequences.[4]

Fig. 1 View of façade from Central Avenue.

The city is in a sense a victim of its own vastness: nowhere in its two thousand square miles[5] has it ever developed a center. The grid only continues to unfold over the desert, subduing and adapting the tractless expanse to Phoenix's "dream of order."[6] Pre-fabricated, planned neighborhoods unfold over the skeleton of numbered streets. The subdivisions and dreaded strip malls stand as an experiment in suburbanism, arising from the quixotic dreams of intruders eager to tame the area and settle the plots to which they feel entitled as if the city's expansion is an exercise in latter-day Manifest Destiny. It is increasingly apparent that this place defies not only explication, but also the standard set of rules that allow sign and signifier to be clearly identified.

In terms of development, Phoenix is a relative latecomer, just beginning to establish its own identity, despite a lack of appropriate examples on which to model itself. Cities in the East, for example, were able to pattern themselves after their European progenitors, but the "tightly woven fabric"[7] of these East Coast settlements would be entirely inappropriate in the desert expanse of Arizona. Even other western cities provide no parallel and no example; to follow developmental patterns similar to those of Los Angeles would be tantamount to "failure" according to Vernon Swaback, a Phoenix urban planner and one-time apprentice to Frank Lloyd Wright.[8] While long established cities struggle to produce growth in moribund districts, newer cities of the southwestern desert hasten to devise ways of coping with the urban explosion.[9]

In the midst of the economic and population boom of the 1980s, Phoenix found itself at a crossroads, grasping for a mature sense of its own evolving identity. It could no longer deny the reality that it had become a major city. Yet, its cultural life, despite the astonishing growth rate, remained more suited to the agrarian outpost it once had been.[10] In the early 1980s, city officials decided to initiate a plan to invigorate downtown through cultural enhancements, with Mayor Terry Goddard stating "No great city exists without a heart, without an active vibrant center."[11] To the surprise of the city council, Phoenix voters approved a one billion dollar bond issue, twenty-five percent of which underwrote a quality of life bill, including a provision for the expansion of the Phoenix Art Museum.[12] A grassroots campaign had managed to marshal enough support not simply to improve the cultural life of the area, but to establish a new identity for the city. Phoenix had made a clear decision that a unified civic experience, specifically a new arts district, would be an integral part of its character in the twenty-first century and a formative influence in the continued development of its nascent sense of self.

This goal forced Phoenix to come to terms with its disdain for the "indoor" nature of cultural life as manifested in established eastern cities,[13] a concept that is either foreign to desert inhabitants or an unpleasant reminder to those who immigrated to the area fleeing such an existence. The geographical component of the region is indeed so strong that it attracts a type, not only retirees and snowbirds seeking refuge in the warmth, but also a particular brand of rugged individualist whose self-concept is bound up in notions of the West as a haven for mavericks. Compounding this sense of independence is Phoenix's staunch resistance to conformity. The lack of a civic precedent derives largely from one difference between Phoenix and other cities: the powerful, inescapable sense of geography, as much phenomenon as physical place. The mountains of the desert are bigger than any building and, as a result, emphasis shifts toward geography and away from the process of becoming a "city" in the orthodox sense. To this end, the city has begun to create and implement a coherent approach to architecture and city planning that takes the desert and mountains into account. In a conscious rejection of the subjugating grid, recent building programs have attempted to form a system of mesa-like constructions, coexisting in pacific bliss with the serene yet rugged terrain.[14] This "holistic approach" to growth makes possible a careful balance between urbanization and nature.[15]

The new art museum, along with several other major civic projects, is a conscious effort by the city to reinvent and redefine itself as a major metropolis while creating a viable downtown district. Museums have, themselves, undergone redefinition in recent years; their role as repositories for the collection, conservation, and exhibition of objects has expanded to include a function as arbiters of civic identity.

Accordingly, a committee was formed to begin the search for an architect who could transform the existing museum building into a distinctive, "progressively classical"[16] structure, not a late 1980s Post-Modern behemoth that would subordinate the collection. With prior experience in museum design, John Meunier, Dean of the School of Architecture at Arizona State University, presented the selection committee with a set of criteria to follow in choosing an architect. It was decided that a deep understanding of the social and physical context of Phoenix as well as a capacity for building "culturally significant artifacts"[17] would weigh heavily in the decision. Less defined but of equal importance is what James Ballinger, Director of the Phoenix Art Museum, calls a "philosophical match." The long and delicate relationship that would ensue between client and architect would result in years of working closely with the museum staff, in a partnership that Ballinger likens to marriage. A majority of the nominees, including such prominent architects as James Sterling and Peter Eisenmann, represented safe, corporate approaches. Ballinger, however, taking no notice of fame or notoriety, insisted that at least one firm be a dark horse. In this way he hoped to offset the commonly held belief that young architects cannot reach true proficiency until later in their careers. He was concerned that the museum renovation would command the complete attention of the selected architect and felt that a large firm would devote only partial effort.[18] Eisenmann especially showed great interest in the project, but it soon became apparent that his exuberant style and paradoxical vocabulary were clearly incongruous with the aims of this unconventional desert museum.[19] In a gesture symbolic of the youthful, rebellious nature of the museum and its frontier hometown, the committee passed over more established firms to select the young, little known New York firm of Tod Williams, Billie Tsien, and Associates.

In keeping with the serene, minimal aesthetic of their work, Williams and Tsien felt an acute sense of obligation to develop a fundamental understanding of the place and the ways in which its inhabitants had learned to build in the desert environs. Taliesin West, Frank Lloyd Wright's utopian desert compound, provided the ultimate example of the integration of architecture and environment. Tsien relates the story of Taliesin's construction in which large desert rocks were carried to the building site by hand in sheets of newspaper. They were then placed lovingly in the concrete one-by-one and, in what seems as though part of a quasi-religious ceremonial act, the newspaper was then lit on fire and burned away. The remarkable respect for the desert surroundings and its majestic power evidenced by this reverent act characterizes the spirit that Williams and Tsien hoped to capture in their design.

Fig. 2 Steel bridge linking the two wings.

With a talent for making beautiful building materials from humble sources and a desire to utilize local industries and practices, the architects chose to enshroud the structure with massive precast concrete panels produced in the area. To counteract—but not deny—the warm colors of the desert, they settled on a palette that echoes the cooler tones occurring in the region. In covering the panels with green quartz (fig. 1), Williams and Tsien formed a conceptual connection to the earthen materials used in Wright's stone and cement construction at Taliesin West. Such harmonious relationships between architecture and the natural environs maintained a position of importance throughout the project.

Equally significant to the architects was the idea that a structure must forge a connection with its social environment. With a large population of newcomers to the city, the museum required that its new building be readily identifiable. A ninety-four-foot-tall conical sculpture pavilion was intended to serve this purpose, providing a much needed recognition factor to the Phoenix skyline. Although still awaiting funding, the cone—when completed—will utilize Middle Eastern techniques for providing a fine, cooling mist and will be illuminated at night, marking the center of what will become the city's arts district.[20] Williams and Tsien also realized that they needed to give the almost invisible extant structure a character of its own. Towards that goal, they built a separate wing (in a former parking lot), which conveys a dynamic sense of movement when viewed from an automobile moving

Fig. 3 Steel bridge linking the two wings.

the architects' use of inclined walks in creative ways that are fully integrated into the design of the building and not simply added on to meet requirements for handicap accessibility (fig. 4). Although it is possible to reach the upstairs galleries by a large elevator located in the foyer outside of the current exhibition gallery, this is not the preferred method of progressing through the space. To Williams, elevators are awkward spaces that he would prefer to "eliminate... from our vocabulary."[25] In contrast to many architects who feel that mundane considerations place limitations on their creative freedom, Williams and Tsien embrace these "issues of esthetics and ethics" in their methodology, avoiding the proclivity of Post-Modern architects for subordinating people within the all-important design scheme.[26] The architect's infamous self-indulgence is curiously absent. In retrospect, it is evident to the visitor that some hand has been at work, but it is an invisible hand. Ironically, for the first time in museum architecture there has been a so-called death of the architect-author.

along Central Avenue.[21] The horizontality of the gleaming steel bridge (figs. 2 and 3) joining the old and new wings will eventually combine with the vertical thrust of the sculpture pavilion to impart a real presence to the museum as a whole, securing its place as the beacon of cultural life that it was intended to be.

The architects sought to continue the symbiosis of the dynamism of the exterior with the ever-present vastness of the desert in their redistribution of the interior spaces. Williams and Tsien planned the journey through the galleries to be a clear and logical progression, while at the same time maintaining the visitor's freedom of movement.[22] Achieving this required a complete reorganization of the original building's hopelessly confusing maze, prompting the architects to aim for an intuitive path that could be understood through "the soles of the feet" rather than the intellect.[23] The result is logical, but in an organic, fluid way. Passageways were designed not only with the usual teleological scheme that gives priority to a clearly seen terminus but also includes the possibility of looking back from that end point to view the beginning.[24] The physical journey through the museum is so instinctive that the exact order of movement is not very memorable, most likely because the architects, in a deliberate echo of the desert's expansiveness, refrain from dictating a specific path. They wanted visitors to develop a familiarity with the space as a result of their own movement through it, following the lead of one's personal inclinations in a meandering trip through the building, rather than be trapped into searching for prescribed pathways. This goal inspired

Fig. 4 Inclined walk.

The museum, with its quietude and paucity of distractions, issues a silent invitation to look, sit, wander, and ponder. The architects strove for serenity, a quality for which their work is known. Although tranquillity pervades the structure, particularly in the interior spaces, surprises do appear unexpectedly in places. Small, oddly positioned windows are situated in unlikely locations, providing the opportunity for personal orientation within the space.[27] The steel bridge opens onto a small upstairs gallery at one end, but on the opposite end leaves the visitor on a cantilever dramatically overlooking the huge Great Hall (fig. 5). The unexpected assertion of space is only partly muted by an inventive lighting system that focuses on the objects while keeping the sensibility of the space tranquil and dim. A vast eighty-four thousand square foot space that allows the museum to display large art works[28]—and provides an area for fundraising and entertainment events,[29]—the Great Hall also currently serves to house part of the twentieth-century collection. More sumptuous materials have been used in the construction of this room, from the sandstone floors to the slabs of green glass that slice through the walls to allow in a minimal amount of the intense Arizona sun.[30]

Fig. 5 Great Hall.

Similar in scale, the Current Exhibition gallery (fig. 6) engages in a dialogue with the Great Hall, while representing an informal, loft-like aesthetic. Its white walls are most likely attributable to the room's function and not to anachronistic attempts to uphold tired ideas of a decontextualized, sacrosanct space for viewing art. The gallery achieves the requisite level of flexibility to accommodate each exhibition through its movable partitions and large rectilinear format. The fact remains, however, that the space serves some artworks better than others. An exhibition of Chinese scholars' rocks clearly illustrates this problem. The intimate scale and muted colors of the objects renders them nearly invisible in the immense, austere white room. The scenario could not be more different in a recent Triennial exhibition of works by contemporary artists. The huge space is enlivened by the diversity of forms, media, and scale that reflects the pervasive stimuli of contemporary society. Clearly, the fact that much artwork produced today is created with the hope that it will eventually find itself in a large, public setting[31] coincides with the intended function of this gallery.

Fig. 6 Current Exhibition gallery

In contrast to the open spaces of the downstairs galleries, which display large modern pieces, the upstairs rooms produce an intimate focus. The overall sense of space is more domestic, with lowered ceilings and carpeted floors. This familiar impression is heightened by the objects displayed in these small galleries—European and Spanish Colonial works, costumes, miniatures, and cowboy art—which once adorned the homes of the city's well-to-do. Each gallery is furnished with benches and built-in bookshelves, intended by the architect to add to the intimate atmosphere. These smaller divisions seem to bring order and a sense of enclosure to the vast, desert-like scale of the galleries in the rest of the museum.

Not all of the museum's renovations have proven as immediately successful. Ballinger foresaw the possibility of the sculpture pavilion becoming a "political firecracker"[32] if taxpayers were charged with funding a ninety-four-foot-high experimental fiberglass cone at a price of $4 million.

Hoping to avoid massive debt and mindful of the difficulty of convincing donors to pay for structures that have already been built,[33] he decided to delay construction of the pavilion until funds were available. Similarly, the museum chose not to take out loans to finish other incomplete areas, notably the twentieth-century gallery, the central courtyard, and the entrance canopy. Uppermost in the decision-making has been the desire never to cheapen, but to retain quality and build as funds became available. Consequently, the museum's intended function as a civic landmark has not yet been fulfilled.

Like its architecture, the Phoenix Art Museum still grapples with an identity in process, its unfinished elements signifying a welcome departure from the traditional tightly controlled Cartesian grid. The building is not an exercise in theoretical experimentation with art for art's sake. Devoid of the ideology that has caused many Post-Modern structures to recede quickly back into history, like relics of the past, it is an example of architecture freed from paralyzing opposites: client/architect, ego/other, East Coast culture/West Coast pretension. Here in the vast expanse of the desert it is an instance of innovation, increasingly impossible within the confines of an established cultural milieu. This area has consistently sponsored significant architecture, from the utopian visions of Frank Lloyd Wright and Paolo Soleri to the progressive ambitions of Antoine Predock and Will Bruder. In this sense, an important part of the identity of Phoenix has already been formed, it simply awaits full recognition.

---

1 Edward Lebow, "Building a Phoenix for the 21st Century," Valley Guide Quarterly (Fall 1996): 75.
2 Bryn Bailer, "Museum Mecca" *Arizona Daily Star*, 6 October 1996, 11.
3 Reed Kroloff, "Phoenix and Urban Renewal," *Architecture* 84 (April 1995): 76-78.
4 Michael Sorkin, "Criticism: Phoenix and the New Phoenix Art Museum," *Architectural Record* 185 (January 1997): 85.
5 Kroloff, 78.
6 Sorkin, 86.
7 Billie Tsien, Tod Williams, Billie Tsien, and Associates, phone interview by author, New York, NY, 1 October 1998.
8 Vernon Swaback, *Designing the Future* (Tempe: Arizona State University, 1997): 7.
9 *Ibid.*, x.
10 Kroloff, 78.
11 *Ibid.*
12 Robert Chamberlain, Director of Development, interview by author, Phoenix, AZ, 26 March 1998.
13 Lebow, 77.
14 Tsien, phone interview.
15 Swaback, x.
16 James Ballinger, Director, Pheonix Art Museum, interview by author, Phoenix, AZ, 26 March 1998.
17 John Meunier, interview by author, Phoenix, AZ, 24 September 1998.
18 Ballinger, interview.
19 Meunier, interview.
20 Ballinger, interview.
21 Wayne Fujii, "Tod Williams and Billie Tsien," *GA Document* 50 (April 1997): 64
22 Freiman, Ziva, "The Brain Exchange," *Progressive Architecture* 76 (April 1995): 77.
23 Tsien, phone interview.
24 Tsien, phone interview.
25 Fujii, 64.
26 *Ibid.*
27 Tsien, phone interview.
28 Phoenix Art Museum Website.
29 Ballinger, interview.
30 Sorkin, 94.
31 Philip Fisher, *Making and Effacing Art: Modern American Art in a Culture of Museums* (New York: Oxford University Press, 1991), 27.
32 Ballinger, interview.
33 Chamberlain, interview.

R. Doss Mabe

The California Science Center: Staying the Course in Exposition Park

The idea of building a museum as the centerpiece in a scheme to enhance and even to regenerate part of the city is not, of course, particularly novel today. It is more than twenty years since the Centre Georges Pompidou opened in the Marais quarter of Paris to great fanfare (arguably more successful as a social center and tourist attraction than as a place to see art), and several of the architectural examples in this exhibition were conceived at least in part with such an urbanistic objective in mind. The reinvention and rebuilding of the somewhat tired California Museum of Science and Industry as the bold new California Science Center, for instance, began with the understanding that its historic setting in Exposition Park also would require much attention. If the new Science Center was to be successful in its old location, in addition to rebuilding itself the institution would have to provide leadership in reversing the physical deterioration of the Park and in restoring its popular image as a safe destination for visitors.

In 1988 the California Museum of Science and Industry began to rethink its role in science education, aiming to create a new paradigm for such institutions. It realized that both the forum and the format for science education were changing: toward emphasis on how individuals learn through the interpretation of their own experiences to derive their own meanings, and toward focus on how hands-on experiences facilitated by educators using new tools and technologies can enhance learning in science. It also realized that its facilities and exhibits were outmoded, at the same time that its potential audience and its educational mission had broadened considerably. Seeking to come to terms with its location in the heart of an extremely cosmopolitan and multicultural city, it redefined its fundamental mission to increase scientific literacy, with the intent of bringing the "wow" as well as the mysteries of contemporary science to a diverse audience, and of reasserting its leadership in informal science education.

Fig. 1 Aerial view of Exposition Park; California Science Center visible above the Coliseum, lower right corner.

By 1990 a new mission statement and the outlines of a building program had been approved by the museum's Board of

Directors, and in that year two of its oldest buildings—the former Agricultural Exposition Building and the former National Guard Armory, both dating back to 1913—were closed to the public for seismic safety reasons, with severe consequences for its educational objectives and its attendance. Since its founding the museum had grown, not to everyone's satisfaction, to occupy eight separate building structures, the latest being Frank Gehry's California Aerospace Museum. The latter, for example, completed in 1984 just prior to the Olympic Games, was never embraced sympathetically by the museum as an exhibition space. In 1991 the museum made the critical decision to rebuild its facilities in Exposition Park and commissioned Zimmer Gunsul Frasca Partnership to prepare a new master plan for the Park and to determine the best site for its new building program of approximately 600,000 square feet. Although led by the California Museum of Science and Industry, this was a broadly conceived, community-based planning effort involving all of the institutions and stakeholders in and around Exposition Park, along with elected officials at city, county, state, and federal levels. Hence, the siting of the museum's proposed new facilities was but one in a series of planning issues, which invoked historic rivalries contesting the use of Exposition Park's limited land area for building, parking, and recreational purposes. The museum found its own future inextricably bound to the success of a renewed Exposition Park, the museum's new facilities would continue to play a leading role in the series of ambitious projects envisioned for the Park and the adjoining neighborhoods in the city. Again and again, in the ensuing years, the museum and its Board of Directors would be called upon to assist in the rebuilding of Exposition Park and its environs.

Fig. 2 California Science Center, interior.

Changing the name of the California Museum of Science and Industry to the California Science Center in 1998 symbolized completion of the institution's efforts to redefine itself, the launch of its new building, and start-up of its new exhibit and educational programs. In recent decades, science centers, especially, have been noted for experimenting with alternative techniques for presentation of cultural information and for exploration of the contemporary conception of the museum as an open and active place. They have grappled with the problem of how to present the almost infinite and always changing world of science in definable and focused "bite-sized chunks." One strategy has been to capitalize upon the high presentation standards of theme parks, while seeking to raise the bar on the level of content in exhibits. They have been transforming themselves from "temples" to "forums" of science, and it was with these developments in mind that the California Science Center decided to present the topic of science through four thematic oriented exhibit programs—

Fig. 3 Main entrance.

designed to break down the traditional institutional barriers that had hitherto compartmentalized scientific inquiry, and to integrate science with the everyday life experiences of its visitors. In the "World of Life" visitors learn how people, plants, animals, and the tiniest living cells perform the same life processes to survive. In the "Creative World" they examine the constructed environments created with the technologies and inventions of humankind. The "World of the Pacific" takes visitors on a journey around the Pacific Rim, focusing on the earth's ecosystems and how they function. Finally, "Worlds Beyond" explores the universe and the craft we have designed to leave the boundaries of the earth itself.

As the site for its new facility, the Science Center chose to retain its historic location between the seven-acre Rose Garden on the north and Coliseum Drive on the south (fig. 1). While the former is much beloved in Los Angeles as the centerpiece of the original Beaux-Arts grouping of Science Center, Natural History Museum, and National Guard Armory (slated to become the Science Center's educational wing which will collaborate with a science-oriented, neighborhood elementary school), the latter offered easy automobile and pedestrian access from the Park's major entrances. Once the existing structures were cleared away, it was reasoned, this central location offered the possibility

Fig. 4 Ahmanson Building, façade.

of an unparalleled sequence of public spaces, beginning with a new street entrance from parking on the south and culminating with views over the Rose Garden and the city on the north. Programmatically, the four "Worlds" of science would be grouped about a central public space, to be called "Science Court," which would also link directly to restaurants, retail shops, meeting rooms, temporary exhibition galleries, and a new IMAX theater.

Only one obstacle remained: what to do about the 1913 Agricultural Exposition Building, now called the Ahmanson Building after one of the Center's principal benefactors. Initially the Science Center intended to completely replace the Ahmanson with the new facility, but the preservation community led by the Los Angeles Conservancy objected strenuously and a compromise was reached. The Conservancy and the California Office of Historic Preservation agreed to the new building program, provided that the north wing facing the Rose Garden would be retained and its north façade, defaced during the 1960s, would be fully restored to its original appearance.

Ironically, following these efforts, the restored north façade and main entrance to the Ahmanson Building, which forms the south wall of the Rose Garden space, is no longer the main entrance to the Science Center. Since most visitors approach the site from Coliseum Drive and parking lots to the south, the Center required a new main entrance from that direction. In response to its situation between Coliseum Drive and the Rose Garden, the new building is composed of five major elements: a freestanding theater cube (rotated 45 degrees from the main building to follow the existing street alignment), a semi-enclosed rotunda (connecting theater and exhibit spaces), the main exhibition block of the Science Center (bisected by a 120-foot-high wedge of skylit space, fig. 2), the 300-foot-long "Science Court," and the restored north wing of the original building. Visitors enter the rotunda and proceed directly to either the theater or the main exhibition building (fig. 3). The Center's ground level houses the retail store, public meeting rooms, and restaurants, and opens up to the skylit wedge of space through which one ascends to the cross-axial "Science Court" overlooking the restaurants and the Rose Garden below. Two of the four themed exhibit areas—"World of Life" and "Creative World"—are represented in the 245,000-square-foot phase one of the Science Center, while the other two are represented today by preview exhibits and will be added in future phases.

The composition of the main building places the anonymous big box of exhibition spaces behind the glass-roofed "galleria" of Science Court. This taut glass element serves

Fig. 5 Entrance pavilion.

as a neutral backdrop for the restored Ahmanson Building which is clad in dark red brick accented by beige terra-cotta (fig. 4). The new, gently-bowed south façade is layered over the exhibition building in a similar manner, and this façade and the cube of the theater are clad in geometric tile patterns that reverse the proportion of red to beige on the historic north façade. In contrast to these richly-colored tile surfaces, the rotunda bares its steel exoskeleton, which is backed by a diaphanous curtain of perforated stainless steel.

Called the Lorsch Family Pavilion, the open-air rotunda is 100 feet in diameter and 88 feet high. Dominating the two triangular spaces of the south-facing Science Plaza where the journey of discovery in the world of science begins for the visitor, it is at once the giant "front porch" of the Science Center and its icon. The public realm of its Plaza is embellished with a family of art works by Washington, DC-based artist Larry Kirkland. The art installations (figs. 5 and 6) are intended to arouse curiosity and to "envelop you in science from the minute you enter the space," say deputy director Ann Muscat and her colleagues. "We wanted the building to be an easy read for our visitors, so that it would be simple for them to figure out where they need to go. We wanted a building that would capture visitors' imaginations—grab their hearts—then we'd go after their minds." The policy of using art to enrich and ennoble the public spaces of the building, as well as to stimulate the visitor's interest in science, is continued in "Science Court" with the kinetic *Hypar* created by Chuck Hoberman of New York. It is this combination of memorable works of art with a generously proportioned spatial sequence that sets apart the Science Center's building from many of its contemporaries in North America. A belief in the importance of public space to the building program, and to a successful visitor experience, connects the Science Center to earlier and more gracious eras of museum-building, when the grand central space was deemed indispensable—for symbolic reasons as much as for visitor orientation purposes. Creating a sense of awe, the "wow" factor, was always one of the Center's objectives in its new facility, and when there was some anxiety on staff about just how grand the building should be because of its proximity to South Los Angeles neighborhoods, area residents stepped in and expressed their own desire for a civic monument in Exposition Park.

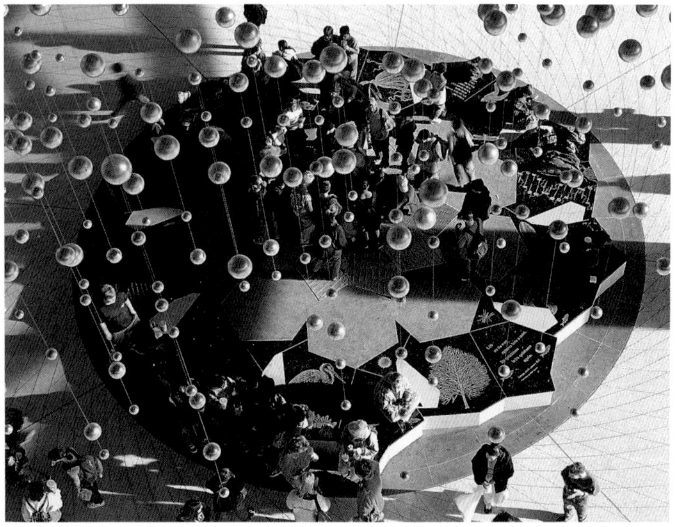

Fig. 6 Gold-and palladium-leaf spheres, installation by Larry Kirkland.

Remarkably the spirit of close collaboration between the Science Center and the surrounding community, which was forged in the initial stages of planning for Exposition Park's future, has endured through a decade of much turbulence in Los Angeles. The successful opening of the Center coincided with phase one improvements to the Park along its deteriorated western edge, and to the landscaping of the Exposition Boulevard median on its northern boundary. During the first year of its operation more than two million visitors have come to the reborn Science Center; and the momentum created by this attendance is spurring other developments in the Park. In addition to the Science Center School and Science Education Resource

Center, plans are being prepared for the Natural History Museum, the California African American Museum, an intergenerational community center, and a second phase of landscaping improvements. Exposition Park is beginning to regain its luster as one of the "crown jewels" of central Los Angeles, so much so that it is now described as the southern anchor to an even more ambitious reinvention of the central city as a truly urban ensemble of sports, entertainment, and cultural facilities lining historic Figueroa Street, punctuated by the Convention Center and the new Staples Center arena, and connecting to the Grand Avenue "arts district" and Dodger Stadium on the north.

If excitement about a renewed central Los Angeles is one factor in the success of the Science Center's new building and exhibit program, the "wow" is also due to its success as an environment for learning about science, not only for kids, but for moms and dads whose interest obviously has been piqued. Although phase one works well enough, the long process of designing, building, and commissioning the operations of the new Center is studded with lessons learned. The eventual planned but as yet unfinished structural addition of phases to the building and, by definition, to the exhibit program will require much collaboration between staff, exhibit designers (such as West Office Design who created phase one), architects, and engineers. As a sequence of public spaces the building needs to be fine-tuned to control and improve visitor circulation in order to handle crowds (up to 15,000 daily) double those projected. Additional vertical circulation will be required, and the staff has asked that the finishes in public spaces be upgraded. The critical question is whether these spaces will adequately support, as intended, the visitor traffic in an expanded building comprising 600,000 square feet of space.

In his insightful *Non-places: Introduction to an Anthropology of Supermodernity,* Marc Augé[1] discusses the meaninglessness of much of the built environment in cities such as Los Angeles. He deplores the trend toward "non-places" such as airports, hotels, supermarkets, and shopping malls where people are thrown together primarily in a sphere of mobility or consumption. He argues that the function of these spaces is quite different in reality from the traditional social centers of communities such as village squares or, perhaps, churches. He contends that the former lack "social meaning" in the classic anthropological sense, because nobody feels any attachment to them. When and where spaces become "places" they acquire meaning as a result of shared human activities, because they are familiar, and because people feel at home in them, while "non-places" serve a highly individuated society where public or semi-public space is seen less as social space than as an area used by everybody individually. Historically, Exposition Park is remembered by many Angelenos as a familiar and inviting place that was lost to a city woefully short of such public places. Perhaps as a result of its repopulation by diverse, multi-ethnic crowds of visitors to the Science Center and its neighboring institutions, the Park will become once again an inviting and familiar alternative to the nearest shopping mall or to the theme park, as a place where people meet each other, talk to each other, and actually share common experiences. The most important measures of success in the Science Center's contribution to the public life in Los Angeles will be both in its encouragement of a renewed interest in scientific culture and in its cultivation of a renewed spirit of community in the heart of the city.

1 Marc Augé, *Non-places: Introduction to an Anthropology of Supermodernity,* trans. John Howe (London, New York: Verso, 1995).

Selected Bibliography

Abrams, Janet. "Contemplation and Congregation in the Popular Urban Art Museum: Two Projects by Venturi, Rauch & Scott-Brown." *Lotus International* 55 (1987): 84-117.

Arata Isozaki: Architecture 1960-1990. Catalogue to Exhibition. New York, Los Angeles: Rizzoli International Publications and Museum of Contemporary Art, 1991.

Barthes, Roland. *Image, Music, Text.* Translated by Stephen Heath. New York: Hill and Wang, 1977.

Berelowitz, Jo-Anne. "From the Body of the Prince to Mickey Mouse." *The Oxford Art Journal* 13, no. 2 (1990): 70-84.

Berelowitz, Jo-Anne. "The Museum of Contemporary Art, Los Angeles: An Account of Collaboration Between Artist, Trustees and an Architect." In *Art Apart: Art Institutions and Ideology Across England and North America.* Edited by Marcia Pointon. Manchester, New York: Manchester University Press, 1994.

Bhabha, Homi. *The Location of Culture.* London: Routledge, 1994.

Burian, Edward R., ed. *Modernity and the Architecture of Mexico.* Austin: University of Texas Press, 1997.

Consejo Nacional para la Cultura y las Artes. *Centro Cultural Tijuana en el centro de la Cultura.* Tijuana, Mexico: Consejo Nacional para la Cultura y las Artes, 1994.

Coolidge, John. *Patrons and Architects: Designing Art Museums in the Twentieth Century.* Forth Worth, Texas: Amon Carter Museum, 1989.

Darragh, Joan and James S. Snyder. *Museum Design, Planning and Building for Art.* New York, Oxford: Oxford University Press in association with American Federation of Arts and National Endowment for the Arts, 1993.

Davies, Hugh M. and Anne Farrell. *Learning from La Jolla: Robert Venturi Remakes a Museum in the Precinct of Irving Gill.* San Diego: Museum of Contemporary Art, San Diego, 1996.

Davis, Douglas. *The Museum Transformed.* New York: Abbeville Press Publishers, 1990.

Duncan, Carol. *Civilizing Rituals: Inside Public Art Museums.* London, New York: Routledge, 1995.

Egan, Timothy. "Venturi's New Seattle Art Museum Opens." *New York Times,* 10 December 1991: Living Arts section.

Failing, Patricia. "Los Angeles Gets a New Temple of Art." *ARTNews* 85 (November 1986): 88-94.

Failing, Patricia. "MOCA: Los Angeles Gets Its Long-awaited Museum of Contemporary Art—or at Least a Temporary Contemporary." *ARTNews*, vol. 82 (October, 1983).

Fisher, Philip. *Making and Effacing Art: Modern American Art in a Culture of Museums.* New York, Oxford: Oxford University Press, 1991.

Flacke, Christopher. "Isozaki's MOCA." *The New Criterion* 5 (April 1987): 46-50.

Frampton, Kenneth. "MOCA, Museum of Contemporary Art, Los Angeles." *Domus* 677 (November 1986): 36-49.

Fujii, Wayne. "Tod Williams and Billie Tsien." *GA Document* 50 (April 1997): 41-91.

Giovannini, Joseph. "Museum Piece." *Art Forum* 25 (February 1987): 3-6.

Goldberger, Paul. "Robert Venturi, Gentle Subverter of Modernism." *New York Times*, 14 April 1991.

Gomez, Gwendolyn and Anne Farrell. "From Theory to Practice: Developing Diversity: Three Case Studies." *Museum News,* May/June 1998.

Greenberg, Reesa, Bruce W. Ferguson, and Sandy Nairne, eds. *Thinking About Exhibitions.* London: Routledge Press, 1996.

Isozaki, Arata. "A Chain of Subtle Changes." *The Japan Architect*, no. 358 (February 1987): 22-23.

Isozaki, Arata. "The Museum of Contemporary Art, Los Angeles." *The Japan Architect*, no. 358 (February 1987): 14-21.

Jameson, Frederic. "Postmodernism and Consumer Society." In *The Anti-Aesthetic: Essays on Postmodern Culture.* Edited by Hal Foster. Port Townsend: Bay Press, 1983.

Jameson, Frederic. *Postmodernism or, the Cultural Logic of Late Capitalism.* Durham: Duke University Press, 1997.

Jencks, Charles A. *The Language of Post-Modern Architecture.* 4th ed. New York: Rizzoli International Publications, 1984.

Jencks, Charles and George Baird, eds. *Meaning in Architecture,* New York: George Braziller, 1969.

Kapplinger, Claus. "Architecture and the Marketing of the Museum." *Museum International*, vol. 49 (October-December 1997).

Kohn, Wendy, ed. *Moshe Safdie.* London: Academy Editions, 1996.

Kroloff, Reed. "Phoenix and Urban Renewal." *Architecture* 84 (April 1995): 77-84

"La Jolla Museum Branches Out." *Architecture* 82 (May 1993): 24.

Lampugnani, V. M. "Venturi, Rauch, Scott Brown: Seattle Art Museum." *Domus* 699 (1988): 36-40.

Lane, John R. *The Making of a Museum.* San Francisco: San Francisco Museum of Modern Art, 1995.

Lavin, Sylvia. "Venturi, Rauch and Scott Brown Disclose the Plans for Three New Museum Projects, Showing Complexity and Tradition in Design for the Viewing of Art." *Interiors* 147 (November 1987): 131-137, 166.

Lutyens: The Work of the English Architect Sir Edwin Lutyens (1869-1944). London: Arts Council of Great Britain, 1981.

Lyotard, Jean-Francois. *The Postmodern Condition: A Report on Knowledge.* Translated by Geoff Bennington and Brian Massumi. Minneapolis: University of Minnesota Press, 1979.

Maxwell, Diane. "Museum of Contemporary Art, San Diego: the New Downtown Building." Museum of Contemporary Art, San Diego News Release, 10 December 1992.

Meier, Richard. *Building the Getty.* New York: Alfred A. Knopf, 1997.

Morgan, Ann Lee and Colin Naylor, eds. *Contemporary Architects.* Chicago: St. James Press, 1987.

Muschamp, Herbert. "The L.A. Museum of Contemporary Art: What's in a Name?" *Architectural Record*, vol. 175 (May 1987).

Mutlow, John V., ed. *Ricardo Legorreta Architects.* New York: Rizzoli International Publications, 1997.

Myers, I. E. *Mexico's Modern Architecture.* New York: Architectural Book Publishing Co., 1952.

Nacher, Yves. "From Medium to Message: Museum Architecture Today." *Museum International*, vol. 49 (October-December 1997).

Newhouse, Victoria. *Towards a New Museum.* New York: Monacelli Press, 1998.

Nicolin, Pierluigi. "The Context as Collage: The Decorative Response of Robert Venturi in Seattle." *Lotus International* 74 (1992): 86-97.

Nicolin, Pierluigi. *Mario Botta: Buildings and Projects 1961-1982.* New York: Rizzoli International Publications, 1984.

O'Connor, Anne-Marie. "Mexico's City of Promise." *Los Angeles Times,* 26 January 1998, sec. A, p. 1, 19.

Oliver, Paul, ed. *Encyclopedia of Vernacular Architecture of the World.* Cambridge: Cambridge University Press, 1997.

Oechslin, Werner and Pierluigi Nicolin. *Mario Botta: Architectures 1980-1990.* Barcelona: Editorial Gustgavo Gili, S.A., 1991.

Ollman, Leah."A Trolley's Eye View." *ARTNews* 92 (September 1993): 26.

Ollman, Leah. "Report From San Diego. A Change of Weather?" *Art in America,* July 1997, 35-43.

Pastier, John. "L.A. Art: Dissimilar Duo. 'Complementary Paradoxes' in the California City's Two New Modern Museums." *Architecture* 76 *(February 1987): 41-53.*

Patton, Phil. "Isozaki: Japan's Best Architect Gives Los Angeles a Great Museum." *Connoisseur* 216 (November 1986): 118-125.

Piano, Renzo and Richard Rogers. *Du Plateau Beaubourg au Centre Georges Pompidou.* Paris: Association des amis du Centre Georges Pompidou and Editions du Centre Georges Pompidou, 1987.

Pizarro, Javier, ed. *Ramírez Vázquez.* Mexico City: Garciá Valades Editores, 1989.

Pizzi, Emilio. *Mario Botta: Works and Projects.* Barcelona: Editorial Gustavo Gili, S.A., 1997.

Plagens, Peter. "Exemplary Contemporary." *Art in America,* March 1984.

Pointon, Marcia, ed. *Art Apart: Art Institutions and Ideology Across England and North America.* Manchester and New York: Manchester University Press, 1994.

Raczka, Robert. "MOCA Sights Local Art in 'Striking Distance'." *New Art Examiner* 15 (June 1988): 39-40.

Ramírez Vázquez, Pedro. "La Arquitectura del Museo Nacional de Antropologia." *Artes de Mexico,* no. 66/67 (1965).

Rich, Andrea. "Educating the Next Generation of Art Lovers." *Los Angeles Times,* 26 October 1997, sec. M, p. 3.

Salguero, Ramon Vargas. *Pabellones y Museos de Pedro Ramírez Vázquez.* Mexico City: Noriega Editores, 1995.

Seal, Margaret. "Phoenix Rising." *Architectural Review* 202 (November 1997): 38-44.

Schmertz, Mildred F. "MOCA and More: The Future of California Plaza at Bunker Hill." *Architectural Record* 175 (May 1987): 82.

Slessor, Catherine. "Breaking The Box." *Architectural Review*, vol. 202 (December 1997).

Sorkin, Michael. "Criticism: Phoenix and the New Phoenix Art Museum." *Architectural Record* 185 (January 1997): 85-97.

Staten, Peter. "Serious Whimsy." *Seattle Weekly*, 11 December 1991.

Steele, James, ed. *Museum Builders.* London: Academy Editions, 1994.

Stein, Karen D. "Irving Gill Reconsidered." *Architectural Record* (August 1996): 88-91.

"Summing Up Venturi." *The Economist,* 7 December 1991, 110.

Temko, Allan. "Art and Soul." *San Francisco Focus,* January 1995.

Trueblood, Beatrice, ed. *Museums 1952-1994: Pedro Ramírez Vázquez.* Translated by Debra Nagao. Texts by Roberto Vallerino. Mexico City: Artes Gráficas Panorama, S.A. de C.V., 1995.

Vanesian, Kathleen. "Sunrise in the Valley." *ARTNews* (January 1997): 43-44.

Venturi, Robert. *Complexity and Contradiction in Architecture.* 2nd ed. New York: Museum of Modern Art, 1977.

Venturi, Robert. "Diversity, Relevance and Representation in Historicism, or Plus C, Change... Plus Ça Plea for Pattern All Over Architecture with a Postscript on My Mother's House." *Architectural Record* (June 1982): 114-119.

Venturi, Robert. Interview by Hugh M. Davies and Ronald J. Onorato. Tape recording, 13 July 1994. Museum of Contemporary Art, San Diego Oral History Collection, La Jolla, Calif.

Venturi, Robert, Denise Scott Brown, and Steven Izenour. *Learning from Las Vegas.* Rev. ed. Cambridge: MIT Press, 1977.

Von Moos, Stanislaus. *Venturi, Rauch & Scott Brown Building Projects.* New York: Rizzoli International Publications, 1987.

Viladas, Pilar. "MOCA Moves In." *Progressive Architecture* 67 (November 1986): 83-95.

Viladas, Pilar. "The Undecorated Shed." *Progressive Architecture,* March 1984.

Vonier, Thomas. "Museum Architecture: The Tension Between Form and Function." *Museum News,* vol. 66 (May/June 1988).

Watari, Etsuko. *Mario Botta: Watari-Um Project in Tokyo 1985-1990.* Tokyo: Watari-Um Museum, 1990.

Williams, Harold M., Ada Huxtable, Stephen D. Rountree, et. al. *Making Architecture: The Getty Center.* Los Angeles: The J. Paul Getty Trust, 1997.

Wilson, William. "Temporary Contemporary: Its Time is Now." *Los Angeles Times,* 20 November 1983: sec. C.

Wrede, Stuart. *Mario Botta.* New York: Museum of Modern Art, 1986.

Photo Credits

California Science Center
All photographs by Timothy Hursley, courtesy of Zimmer, Gunsul, Frasca Partnership

The Getty Center
Fig. 1 Photograph by Charles A. Lagreco
Fig. 2 Photograph by Charles A. Lagreco
Fig. 3 Photograph by Julius Shulman
Fig. 4 Photograph by Charles A. Lagreco
Fig. 5 Photograph by Charles A. Lagreco
Fig. 6 Photograph by Charles A. Lagreco

Museum of Contemporary Art, Los Angeles
Fig. 1 Courtesy of The Museum of Contemporary Art
Fig. 2 Photograph by Gene Ogami
Courtesy of The Museum of Contemporary Art
Fig. 3 Photograph by Tim Street-Porter
Courtesy of The Museum of Contemporary Art
Fig. 4 Courtesy of Centre Georges Pompidou
Fig. 5 Courtesy of The Museum of Contemporary Art
Fig. 6 Photograph by Michael Moran
Courtesy of The Museum of Contemporary Art

Museum of Contemporary Art, San Diego (Downtown)
Fig. 1 Photograph by Glenn Cormier
Courtesy of Museum of Contemporary Art, San Diego
Fig. 2 Photograph by Glenn Cormier
Courtesy of Museum of Contemporary Art, San Diego
Fig. 3 Courtesy of David Raphael Singer, Architect
Fig. 4 Courtesy of David Raphael Singer, Architect
Fig. 5 Courtesy of Museum of Contemporary Art, San Diego
Fig. 6 Courtesy of San Diego Museum of Art

Museum of Contemporary Art, San Diego (La Jolla)
Fig. 1 Photograph by Timothy Hursley © 1996
Courtesy of Museum of Contemporary Art, San Diego
Fig. 2 Photograph by Timothy Hursley
Courtesy of Museum of Contemporary Art, San Diego
Fig. 3 Photograph by Timothy Hursley © 1996
Courtesy of Museum of Contemporary Art, San Diego
Fig. 4 Photograph by Timothy Hursley © 1996
Courtesy of Museum of Contemporary Art, San Diego
Fig. 5 Courtesy of Venturi, Scott Brown and Associates
Fig. 6 Photograph by Timothy Hursley © 1996
Courtesy of Museum of Contemporary Art, San Diego

Phoenix Art Museum
All photographs courtesy of Tod William, Billie Tsien, and Associates

San Francisco Museum of Modern Art
Fig. 1 Photograph by Richard Barnes
Courtesy of San Francisco Museum of Modern Art
Fig. 2 Photograph by Nan Park
Courtesy of San Francisco Museum of Modern Art
Fig. 3 Photograph by Richard Barnes
Courtesy of San Francisco Museum of Modern Art
Fig. 4 Photograph by Nan Park
Fig. 5 Photograph by Nan Park

Seattle Art Museum
Fig. 1 Photograph by Matt Wargo
Courtesy of Venturi, Scott Brown and Associates
Fig. 2 Photograph by Matt Wargo
Courtesy of Venturi, Scott Brown and Associates
Fig. 3 Courtesy of Venturi, Scott Brown and Associates
Fig. 4 Photograph by Matt Wargo
Courtesy of Venturi, Scott Brown and Associates
Fig. 5 Photograph by Susan Dirk
Courtesy of Seattle Art Museum
Fig. 6 Photograph by Matt Wargo
Courtesy of Venturi, Scott Brown and Associates

Skirball Cultural Center
Fig. 1 Photograph by Timothy Hursley
Courtesy of Skirball Cultural Center
Fig. 2 Photograph by and courtesy of Timothy Hursley
Fig. 3 Photograph by Timothy Hursley
Courtesy of Skirball Cultural Center
Fig. 4 Photograph by Grant Mudford
Courtesy of Skirball Cultural Center
Fig. 5 Photograph by Timothy Hursley
Courtesy of Skirball Cultural Center
Fig. 6 Photograph by Grant Mudford
Courtesy of Skirball Cultural Center

The Temporary Contemporary (The Geffen Contemporary)
Fig. 1 Courtesy of The Museum of Contemporary Art
Fig. 2 Photograph by Janice Felgar, 1982
Courtesy of Museum of Contemporary Art
Fig. 3 Photograph by Suidd & Nunns
Courtesy of The Museum of Contemporary Art
Fig. 4 Courtesy of The Museum of Contemporary Art
Fig. 5 Photograph by Lyle Ashton Harris
Courtesy of The Museum of Contemporary Art
Fig. 6 Photograph by Dirk Reinartz
Courtesy of The Museum of Contemporary Art

Tijuana Cultural Center
All photographs and drawings courtesy of Manuel Rosen Architects, FAIA

When The Museums Were White:
A Study of the Museum as Building Type
Fig. 1 Courtesy of The Museum of Contemporary Art
Fig. 2 Courtesy of The Museum of Contemporary Art
Fig. 3 Courtesy of Getty Research Institute, Research Library
Fig. 4 Courtesy of Getty Research Institute, Research Library
Fig. 5 Photograph by Marcherita, Spiluttini, Vienna

Cover
Getty Center, photograph by Tommy Chan